Church Year

Series B
Advent • Christmas • Epiphany

Study Guide

By Thomas J. Rogers

Edited by Thomas J. Doyle

Write to the Library for the Blind, 1333 S. Kirkwood Road, St. Louis, MO 63122-7295 to obtain this study in braille or large print for the visually impaired.

Contents

Introduction

About the Series

This course is one of 12 in the Church Year series. The Bible studies in this series are tied to the 3-year lectionary. These studies give participants the opportunity to explore the Old Testament lesson (or lesson from the book of Acts during the Easter season), the Epistle lesson, and the Gospel lesson appointed for each Sunday of the church year. Also, optional studies give participants the opportunity to study in-depth the lessons appointed for festivals that fall on days other than Sunday (e.g., Ascension, Reformation, Christmas, Christmas Eve, Maundy Thursday, Good Friday, Epiphany).

Book 1 for years A, B, and C in the lectionary series will include 17 studies for the Scripture lessons appointed for the Sundays and festival days in Advent, Christmas, and Epiphany. Book 2 will include 17 studies for the lessons appointed for the Sundays and festival days in Lent and Easter and of lessons appointed for Ascension and Pentecost. Book 3 (15 sessions) and 4 (15 sessions) for years A, B, and C will include studies that focus on the lessons appointed for the Pentecost season.

After a brief review and study of the Scripture lessons appointed for a Sunday or festival day, each study is designed to help participants draw conclusions about each of the lessons, compare the lessons, discover a unifying theme in the lessons (if possible), and apply the theme to their lives. At the end of each study, the Scripture lessons for the next Sunday and/or festival day are assigned in preparation for the next study. The Leaders Guide for each course provides additional information on appointed lessons, answers to the questions in the Study Guide, a suggested process for teaching the study, and devotional or worship activities tied to the theme.

May the Holy Spirit richly bless you as you study God's Word!

Session 1

First Sunday in Advent

Isaiah 63:16b–17, 64:1–8; 1 Corinthians 1:3–9;
Mark 13:33–37

Focus

Theme: *Strong to the End*

Law/Gospel Focus

Sinful humans have not lived as God desires. We experience conflict, disappointment, frustration, and disease as a result of sin. But God loves us and sent Jesus to suffer the punishment for our sin on a cross. Jesus will come again to judge the living and the dead. Those who possess saving faith Jesus will judge "Not guilty" and will take to heaven. In heaven we will no longer experience sin and its results. Through Word and Sacrament the Holy Spirit works to keep us strong in the faith as we await Judgment Day in joyful anticipation.

Objectives

By the power of the Holy Spirit working through God's Word we will

1. affirm that Jesus will return to take all who possess saving faith to heaven;
2. rejoice and look forward to Jesus' second coming;
3. live as God's people, who wait in anxious anticipation of Jesus' return to earth.

Opening Worship

Leader: Sing to the LORD a new song, for He has done marvelous things! (Psalm 98:1)

Sing or speak together "Once He Came in Blessing" (*LW* 30).

Once He came in blessing,
All our sins redressing;
Came in likeness lowly,
Son of God most holy;
Bore the cross to save us;
Hope and freedom gave us.

Still He comes within us;
Still His voice would win us
From the sins that hurt us;
Would to truth convert us
From our foolish error
Ere He comes in terror.

Thus, if we have known Him,
Not ashamed to own Him,
Nor have spurned Him coldly
But will trust Him boldly,
He will then receive us,
Heal us, and forgive us.

Those who then are loyal
Find a welcome royal.
Come, then, O Lord Jesus,
From our sins release us;
Let us here confess You
Till in heav'n we bless You.

Leader: Sing to the LORD a new song, for He has done
marvelous things!

Introduction

People love to have things to look forward to. Birthdays, vacations, and Christmas are times that we can look forward to. Unfortunately, the actual celebration of our birthdays, the experiences we have on our vacations, and the way things go at Christmas often disappoint us. Years ago Peggy Lee sang a depressing song about the futility of life. The futility was summed up with these words, "Is that all there is? Is that all there is? If that's all there is my friend than let's keep dancing.

Let's break out the booze and have a ball, if that's all there is."

Our lessons for this Sunday remind us that when the events of this life disappoint us, and when the events of this life delight us, we still have more to look forward to—eternal life in heaven. Because no one knows when the Lord may come back to claim us, we can believe that every day may be that day. This gives every day a chance to be a day full of promise. Each day then has purpose. It leads us one day closer to the perfection we will experience as we live each day with Christ in heaven. In order to praise Jesus, who will come to take us to eternal joy, we can live our lives on earth filled with acts of love and selflessness that invite the whole world to see the coming Jesus in us.

1. What evidence is there in this world that many people don't believe in Judgment Day, a day that will require each person to give a personal accounting of his or her life?

2. Mark reminds us in the Gospel lesson, "Be on guard! Be alert!" for the end is coming. What evidence can you provide that at times even Christians are not on guard or alert?

3. Jesus said, "You do not know when that time will come." Because we do not know the time of His return, Jesus warns, "Be on guard! Be alert!" What does Jesus mean by these words?

<hr>

Inform

Consider the following summaries of the lessons assigned for the First Sunday of Advent.

Isaiah 63:16b–17, 64:1–8—Isaiah addresses the people of Israel and shares with them the Lord's disappointment with their unfaithfulness. They haven't looked like or behaved like the chosen people of God. The people of Israel can't change on their own, but God can and will bring change to Israel and the whole world. Isaiah acknowledges God as the potter and the people of Israel as the clay. Only the potter can transform the clay. A day is coming when all the world will see His glory and turn to Him.

1 Corinthians 1:3–9—St. Paul continues with the theme of the Second Coming. Given the imminent return of Christ, Paul reminds the Corinthian Christians that as they await eagerly Jesus' return that He will keep them strong in the faith until the end. Paul emphasizes God's work in keeping them steadfast in the faith until the day when they through faith will be judged blameless. Our lives centered in Christ allow others to see Him in us and believe in Him as their Savior so that they can also welcome Him with joy when He comes at the end of time.

Mark 13:33–37—Jesus Himself speaks about His return to earth. He reminds His disciples to "Be on guard! Be alert!" Using a metaphor of a man leaving his house and putting his servants in charge, He tells His disciples to "Keep watch because you do not know when the owner of the house will come back." In these words Jesus prepares His disciples for both the time when He will leave them and the time when He will return.

1. What words and/or phrases does Isaiah use to describe the Israelites' relationship to God? God's relationship to the Israelites?

2. What hope does Isaiah still hold in spite of the Israelites' rebellion against God? See Isaiah 64:8.

3. Jesus' words to His disciples, "Be on guard! Be alert!" echo God's continual reminders throughout the Old Testament to the people of Israel. How did the people of Israel respond to God's warnings and pleas? Refer to the Old Testament reading for insight. How do you think the disciples would respond if left to their own devices?

4. Paul says with confidence, "He [Jesus] will keep you strong to the end, so that you will be blameless on the day of our Lord Jesus." How can Paul speak with such confidence? See 1 Corinthians 1:4–6. What confidence do these words give you as you anticipate Judgment Day?

Connect

1. How do the words of Isaiah 64:8 and 1 Corinthians 1:3–9 provide you with confidence, as you respond to Jesus' words, "Be on guard! Be alert!"?

2. The Holy Spirit works through the means of grace—God's Word and Sacraments—to strengthen our saving faith in Jesus. How might seizing opportunities to hear God's Word and celebrate the Lord's Supper better equip us to "Be on guard! Be alert!"? What danger do people risk if they neglect or ignore the means of grace that God has provided? In what activities might you and your family become involved so that God can enable you to be "strong to the end"?

3. People often spend inordinate amounts of time trying to determine the exact time of Jesus' return. Based upon the lessons for today, answer the following questions. Why is trying to determine the time of Jesus' return a futile activity? How might Christians better spend their time to prepare for Christ's return?

====================== **Vision** ======================

During This Week

1. Make a list of all the things you would do today if you knew that the Lord was coming back tomorrow.
2. Make a list of goals that you would like to meet between now and Christ's coming. Then ask yourself, "What must I do today in order to make sure I meet these goals?" Then, go begin doing those things.
3. Name someone you know who doesn't believe in Jesus. Pray daily for that person's salvation.

Closing Worship

Pray or sing together "I'm But a Stranger Here" (*LW* 515).

> I'm but a stranger here, Heav'n is my home;
> Earth is a desert drear, Heav'n is my home.
> Danger and sorrow stand Round me on ev'ry hand;
> Heav'n is my fatherland, Heav'n is my home.
>
> What though the tempest rage, Heav'n is my home;
> Short is my pilgrimage, Heav'n is my home;
> And time's wild wintry blast Soon shall be overpast;
> I shall reach home at last, Heav'n is my home.
>
> Therefore I murmur not, Heav'n is my home;
> Whate'er my earthly lot, Heav'n is my home;
> And I shall surely stand There at my Lord's right hand.
> Heav'n is my fatherland, Heav'n is my home.

Scripture Lessons for Next Sunday

In preparation for the Second Sunday in Advent read Isaiah 40:1–11; 2 Peter 3:8–14; Mark 1:1–8.

Session 2

Second Sunday in Advent

Isaiah 40:1–11; 2 Peter 3:8–14; Mark 1:1–8

Focus

Theme: *Comfort and Confidence*

Law/Gospel Focus

God's Word spoken by Moses and the prophets brought a word of judgment to disobedient people. The Word made flesh, Jesus Christ brings forgiveness and life.

Objectives

By the power of the Holy Spirit working through God's Word we will

1. recognize that without Jesus all people are doomed to eternal death;
2. confess that God did not give up on sinners, but instead sent His only-begotten Son, Jesus, to suffer and die for their sins so that they might receive eternal life;
3. affirm that God in Christ enables people to live in harmony with Him and one another even now as we wait for the attainment of complete harmony in heaven.

Opening Worship

Leader: May the words of my mouth and the meditation of my heart be pleasing in Your sight, O Lord, my Rock and my Redeemer.

Participants: Glory be to the Father and to the Son and to the Holy Spirit; as it was in the beginning, is now, and will be forever. Amen.

Speak or sing "On Jordan's Bank the Baptist's Cry" (*LW* 14).

On Jordan's bank the Baptist's cry
Announces that the Lord is nigh;

Awake and hearken for He brings
Glad tidings of the King of kings!

Then cleansed be ev'ry life from sin;
Make straight the way for God within,
And let us all our hearts prepare
For Christ to come and enter there.

We hail You as our Savior, Lord,
Our refuge and our great reward;
Without Your grace we waste away
Like flow'rs that wither and decay.

Stretch forth Your hand, our health restore,
And make us rise to fall no more;
Oh, let Your face upon us shine
And fill the world with love divine.

Leader: May the words of my mouth and the meditation of my heart, be pleasing in Your sight, O LORD, my Rock and my Redeemer. (Psalm 19:14)
Participants: Amen.

Introduction

A man wandered into a park early one Saturday morning. He was attracted by the noise made by the participants and observers of a Little League baseball team. The man walked toward the game to get a better look at what was causing all the commotion. As he approached, he saw a very little guy sitting on the bench, cheering on his teammates. "Way to go Johnny. Let's get'um David. Hang in there guys." The man determined that because of the boy's enthusiasm his team must be winning by a large margin. So he asked the boy what the score was. The boy looked a little defensive as he said, "Score's 14 to nothing, *them!*" His answer surprised the man. He looked at the little boy and said, "Then young man, how can you be so excited if you're getting beat so badly?" The boy looked at him in disbelief and said, "Mister, we haven't even been up to bat yet."

14

The young man lived with incredible hope. Such is the message of these three lessons. We live by incredible hope rooted and grounded in God's grace through faith in Jesus. War, famine, injustice, and pestilence seem to surround us. But our God reigns, and our God will save His people. "Every valley shall be raised up, every mountain and hill made low; … the rugged places a plain. And the glory of the Lord will be revealed, and all mankind together will see it." Jesus brings the power of love to make those changes happen. Since Jesus has been raised from the dead, there is no such thing as a lost cause for the people of God. There is always hope! "We haven't even been up to bat yet!"

1. Isaiah tells the people of Israel that their nation has been chopped down by sin. What do we as the people of God through faith in Jesus have in common with the little boy at the Little League game?

2. How can we demonstrate hope in a world devastated by sin with the confidence of the boy sitting on the bench, watching his team lose?

3. How might others respond to our confidence?

<hr>

Inform

Consider the following summaries of the lessons assigned for the Second Sunday in Advent.

Isaiah 40:1–11—The prophet informs Israel that despite her apostasy she still enjoys the love and favor of God. That love and favor works itself out in a powerful way as God will raise up a Savior, even from the dead stump of sinful Israel. Jesus will come to those who have turned from God, forgive them, and carry them close to His heart. God will reveal His glory to all people by the forgiveness He provides through His Son, our Savior Jesus.

2 Peter 3:8–14—Peter reminds his audience that God remains faithful to His promises. Jesus will return and with His return those who possess saving faith can look "forward to a new heaven and a new earth, the home of the righteousness." Peter urges the people to remain steadfast in the faith until the day when Jesus returns.

Mark 1:1–8—John the Baptizer comes to the people of Israel with Good News. Although he looks as though he stands in the tradition of those ancient prophets that proclaimed the imminent destruction of Israel because of its sin, John instead brings Good News. There is hope for Israel and the world. John preaches repentance for the forgiveness of sins as he prepares the way for Jesus, "One more powerful than I, the thongs of whose sandals I am not worthy to stoop down and untie."

1. How did Jesus demonstrate throughout His ministry "comfort" to God's people?

2. How does Christ bring comfort to God's people? How does God reveal His glory through the comfort Jesus provides?

3. How do Peter's words provide comfort to God's people?

4. How does Mark 1:1 summarize the comfort God provides to His people? How are these words a summary of all the words that Mark writes thereafter?

16

Connect

1. The comfort that Christ brings enables us to provide comfort to others. How might the God-given ability to comfort one another as Christ comforted us affect our congregations?

2. Jesus came to declare that God provides comfort to all, including the Gentiles. No one ever expected that comfort could be provided to the likes of them. Are there people today who might be considered modern-day "Gentiles," to whom no one would expect God to provide comfort?

3. One characteristic that seems to identify American young people between 18 and 30 is that they have little hope for the future. How do the words of Isaiah speak to them? How might the forgiveness of sins and eternal life Jesus won for them on the cross enable them to live with the confidence of the young boy who proclaimed, "We haven't even been up to bat yet"?

4. What attitudes and behaviors characterize the lives of those who are hopeless? What are the attitudes and behaviors that characterize the lives of those who live in confidence, the comfort about which each of the three lessons speak?

5. It must have been lonely for John the Baptist to be a voice of one calling in the desert. What principles and values do Christians proclaim today that might cause us also to feel like voices calling in the desert?

During this Week

1. Recall times in your life when the Lord has provided you comfort
   and confidence in the midst of what seemed like a wilderness.
   Praise Him for the confidence and comfort He provided.
2. The Pharisees and Sadducees believed that they were "better"
   than Gentiles and other people. John declared that this was not
   true, and he called on them to repent. Make a list of the phari-
   saical tendencies that exist in your life and ask God to forgive you
   and change you.
3. Recall a relationship in your life that has been harmed by selfishness. Ask God to help you reconcile with that person and take
   steps to make that reconciliation possible.

Closing Worship (Psalm 19:1–9)

Leader: "The heavens declare the glory of God; the skies proclaim the
work of His hands."

Participants: "Day after day they pour forth speech; night after night
they display knowledge."

Leader: "There is no speech or language where their voice is not
heard."

Participants: "Their voice goes out into all the earth, their words to
the ends of the world."

Leader: "In the heavens He has pitched a tent for the sun, which is
like a bridegroom coming forth from his pavilion, like a
champion rejoicing to run his course."

Participants: "It rises at one end of the heavens and makes its circuit
to the other; nothing is hidden from its heat."

Leader: "The law of the LORD is perfect, reviving the soul. The statutes
of the LORD are trustworthy, making wise the simple."

Participants: "The precepts of the Lord are right, giving joy to the
heart."

All: "The commands of the LORD are radiant, giving light to the eyes. The fear of the LORD is pure, enduring forever." Glory be to the Father and to the Son and to the Holy Spirit; as it was in the beginning, is now, and will be forever. Amen.

Scripture Lessons for Next Sunday

Read in preparation for the Third Sunday in Advent Isaiah 61:1–3, 10–11; 1 Thessalonians 5:16–24; John 1:6–8, 19–28.

Session 3

Third Sunday in Advent

Isaiah 61:1–3, 10–11; 1 Thessalonians 5:16–24;
John 1:6–8, 19–28

Theme: *God Has Won*

Law/Gospel Focus

Sin has brought desolation to our land, our bodies, and our lives. God has come to our rescue. He sent Jesus to forgive our sin and give us the promise of a new life in heaven.

Objectives

By the power of the Holy Spirit working through God's Word we will

1. understand that with the coming of Christ God ushered us into a new age, a last age where we wait patiently until He will come again to take us to heaven;
2. affirm steadfastness as a necessary part of Christian life in these latter days;
3. find comfort in knowing that God through faith strengthened by the Holy Spirit working through the means of grace makes His people strong to face any crisis or challenge and so enables them to be joyful always; pray continually; and give thanks in all circumstances.

Opening Worship

Sing or speak together the following stanzas from "Oh, Come, Oh, Come, Emmanuel" (*LW* 31).

Oh, come, oh, come, Emmanuel,
And ransom captive Israel,
That mourns in lonely exile here

Until the Son of God appear.
Rejoice! Rejoice! Emmanuel
Shall come to you, O Israel!

Oh, come, O Rod of Jesse's stem,
From ev'ry foe deliver them
That trust Your mighty pow'r to save;
Bring them in vict'ry through the grave.
Rejoice! Rejoice! Emmanuel
Shall come to you, O Israel!

Oh, come, our Dayspring from on high,
And cheer us by Your drawing nigh;
Disperse the gloomy clouds of night,
And death's dark shadows put to flight.
Rejoice! Rejoice! Emmanuel
Shall come to you, O Israel!

Oh, come, Desire of nations, bind
In one the hearts of all mankind;
Oh, bid our sad divisions cease,
And be Yourself our King of Peace.
Rejoice! Rejoice! Emmanuel
Shall come to you, O Israel!

Then pray together,

Father in heaven, You sent Your Son, Jesus, to be our Savior born humbly in Bethlehem. You will send Him again at the time You have appointed to come to take us all home to heaven. Until that time, strengthen us so that with strong arms and voices we can proclaim Your saving name to all the world. Amen.

Introduction

In the Winter Olympics of 1980 The United States had a phenomenal hockey team. They accomplished what many thought was impossible—they won the gold medal. In order to win the gold medal they had to defeat some powerful teams from Czechoslovakia, Canada, and the Soviet Union. Their game against the Soviet Union was

21

televised across the country. People crowded around television sets everywhere to see if the United States could perform a miracle. It was a very close game, with the lead changing hands several times. Because of the difficulties involved in televising such a wonderful event, the picture was broadcast to the United States on a 20-minute delay. That meant that if someone wanted to keep up with the game as it was actually taking place, he or she would have to listen to it on the radio.

Four friends gathered to watch the game on television. As the lead changed hands they got more and more emotional, sometimes ecstatic, sometimes frustrated. As the game was coming to an end, and still it could be won by either side, two of the men, exhausted from the emotion of it all, announced to their friends that they were going to listen to the game on the radio and find out who won. They just couldn't take it any more. The other two men told them not to tell them who won.

About 10 minutes later the two men who had consulted the radio came back into the room. The TV watchers immediately told them to keep their mouths closed. They didn't want to know who won until they saw it for themselves. The two who learned how the game had ended promised to sit silently.

Although they did sit silently, it didn't take long for them to let their friends know that the United States had in fact won. The way they reacted to the game gave away the secret.

It's the same thing for Christians. Ever since Jesus' death and resurrection we have known how all things will work out. God won; we win; we have nothing to fear. We may have trials and setbacks, but we have nothing to fear. That's the message these lessons bring to us.

1. How can people tell by your words and actions that you know God has won for us?

2. Share a time when you or someone you know acted as if God had not won.

3. Because we are in Christ we cannot lose. Satan and the world
    wants us to question and doubt that statement. Share some Bible
    passages that remind us that the victory is ours.

Inform

Here are summaries of the lessons appointed for the Third Sunday of Advent.

Isaiah 61:1–3, 10–11—The prophet Isaiah speaks of the Messianic servant who will come to bind up the brokenhearted, proclaim freedom for captives, and release for the prisoners from darkness. The Messiah will bring salvation to all people, breaking loose the bonds of sin and Satan. Righteousness and praise will spring up to all nations.

1 Thessalonians 5:16–24—Paul informs the early church how they are to live as they await the return of the Lord. Patience coupled with steadfastness will allow the believers to show Jesus to the whole world. Because of what God has done for them in Christ Jesus, Paul urges the Thessalonians to "be joyful always; pray continually; give thanks in all circumstances."

John 1:6–8, 19–28—John the Baptizer was sent by God into this world to testify to the Light of the world, Jesus Christ. When questioned by the Jews, John confessed who he is, who he is not, and who Jesus is. The day after John was questioned by the Jews, he saw Jesus coming toward him and proclaimed, "Look, the Lamb of God, who takes away the sin of the world" (John 1:29).

1. According to Isaiah what will the Messiah provide to those broken by sin and the world?

2. What words of Isaiah indicate that the Messiah will come to save all people, including Gentiles?

3. How did Jesus fulfill the passages of Isaiah during His earthly ministry?

4. How did John's testimony set the stage for the Lamb of God who takes away the sin of the world?

5. Humanly speaking, how might John's testimony been difficult to give?

6. The Thessalonians knew and affirmed that God had won the victory for them through Jesus. Although they had the victory, they still witnessed the effects of sin in the world and were tempted by Satan. In a sense they lived in a "now" and "not yet" state. What did they have "now"? "not yet"?

7. As people possessing saving faith in Jesus, Paul urges the Thessalonians to respond to this good news by demonstrating joy, giving thanks, and praying continually. How do these responses separate the Christian from the unbeliever? How might unbelievers respond to Paul's urging?

1. A Lutheran pastor who had suffered from polio when he was a child walked with a limp. He once was approached by a Pentecostal minister who wanted to "lay hands" on him so that he could be healed. For the Pentecostal minister being healed meant that the pastor wouldn't limp anymore. He approached the Lutheran pastor several times over a period of months. It got to the point that when the Lutheran minister saw the Pentecostal minister coming he would turn the other way. Finally the Lutheran minister said to the Pentecostal, "Friend, I appreciate your concern for my well-being, but I want you to know what I believe about healing. I believe that I am baptized; therefore, I am healed regardless of how I walk." Comment on the pastor's words in light of these lessons.

2. A Japanese Christian lost a teenage daughter in a horrible accident. Her family and church were devastated by this tragedy. After her funeral service, which took place by the side of her grave, her father bent over and picked up three clods of dirt from the pile of dirt next to the grave. He then threw the clods of dirt one at a time onto his daughter's coffin and each time shouted the word, "Banzai! Banzai! Banzai!" This word means victory! Comment on this word in light of 1 Thessalonians 5:16–24.

3. An elder of a Lutheran church approached his pastor with a concern. He wondered why the new members of their congregation almost never attended voters' meetings. He assumed it was because they didn't care about the affairs of the congregation. After a few uncomfortable moments, the pastor responded with these words, "They may not come because I don't encourage them to come. In fact, I sort of discourage them from coming." The shocked elder asked why? The pastor replied that young Christians get really confused when they watch other Christians

argue and grumble against each other. How important are the words of 1 Thessalonians for the health of Christian congregations?

4. A few years ago General Motors released a commercial for it's Buick automobiles. The slogan said, "Buy a Buick and enjoy life. After all, life is to be enjoyed." What would Isaiah, Paul, and John the Baptist say to such a statement?

5. We, like the Thessalonians, live in the "now" and "not yet" era. How? We know what is ahead for us. How does focusing on Jesus' victory enable us to respond as Paul suggests in 1 Thessalonians 5:16–18? How might this enable us to witness our faith to unbelievers?

<hr>

Vision

During This Week

1. Pay attention to the number of times you sigh or complain this week. Carry a notepad with you and write down the reason for the sigh or complaint. Make that list your prayer list for a week. Conclude your prayer each night with the words of Romans 8:31–39.

2. Think about one circumstance in your life that causes you to lose patience. If you find yourself in that situation this week, remember that you are a child of God and an heir of heaven. Recall that you will spend eternity in perfect peace, and then ask yourself, "In light of this, what is my hurry?" And remember your patience glorifies God and serves as "proof" of His presence in your life.

Closing Worship

Sing or speak together "In You Is Gladness" (*LW* 442).

In You is gladness Amid all sadness,
Jesus, sunshine of my heart.
By You are given The gifts of heaven,
You the true Redeemer are.
Our souls are waking;
Our bonds are breaking.
Who trusts You surely
Has built securely
And stands forever. Alleluia!
Our hearts are pining
To see Your shining,
Dying or living To You are cleaving
Now and forever. Alleluia!

If He is ours, We fear no powers,
Not of earth or sin or death.
He sees and blesses
In worst distresses;
He can change them with a breath.
Wherefore the story
Tell of His glory
With hearts and voices;
All heav'n rejoices
In Him forever. Alleluia!
We shout for gladness,
Win over sadness,
Love Him and praise Him
And still shall raise Him
Glad hymns forever. Alleluia!

Scripture Lessons for Next Sunday

Read in preparation for the Fourth Sunday in Advent 2 Samuel 7:(1–7) 8–11, 16; Romans 16:25–27; Luke 1:26–38.

Fourth Sunday in Advent

2 Samuel 7:(1–7) 8–11, 16; Romans 16:25–27; Luke 1:26–38

Focus

Theme: *No More Mystery—God's Way*

Law/Gospel Focus

In His Word God demands that His people be perfect because He is perfect. When His people are not perfect, God has the perfect right to destroy them. But He doesn't. Instead, He reveals to us in His Word a mystery—He came among His sinful people to love and save them through His Son, Jesus. Jesus' death on the cross makes us who once were God's enemies sons and daughters who possess our Father's inheritance—eternal life with Him in heaven. Because of His love we serve Him by what we do and say.

Objectives

By the power of the Holy Spirit working through God's Word we will

1. understand that God transforms human beings separated from Him by sin through Jesus' death on the cross, enabling them to serve Him;
2. realize that God is always working in this world whether we recognize it or not;
3. acknowledge that God is in control of all human history and that He uses those whom He has redeemed through Jesus' blood to serve Him in unique ways;
4. recognize and rejoice in God's constant presence among us.

Opening Worship

Pray together the following prayer:
Leader: Father, today we will face

Participants: Danger, disappointment, frustration, and fear
All: Lord be with us.
Leader: Father, our adversary the devil prowls around like a lion
Participants: seeking someone to devour.
All: Lord be with us.
Leader: Father, cars drive into bridges, our airplanes some-
    times crash to the ground.
Participants: Healthy people come down with catastrophic dis-
    eases.
All: Lord be with us.
Leader: There are those among us who face death,
Participants: And those among us who are called to care for
    them in their last hours; for some, last hours filled with pain.
All: Lord be with us.
Leader: Lord be with us and bless us.
Participants: Amen.

Sing or speak together the following stanzas of "Oh, Come,
Oh, Come, Immanuel" (*LW* 31).

Oh, come, oh, come, Emmanuel,
And ransom captive Israel,
That mourns in lonely exile here
Until the Son of God appear.
Rejoice! Rejoice! Emmanuel shall come to You, O Israel.

Oh, come, Desire of nations, bind
In one the hearts of all mankind;
Oh, bid our sad divisions cease,
And be Yourself our King of Peace.
Rejoice! Rejoice! Emmanuel shall come to You, O Israel.

Introduction

A pastor took a much deserved vacation with his family. They trav-
eled to a family reunion in the Midwest. On the day of the family
reunion, the pastor received word that the police department in his
small town was trying to get in touch with him. He called the police
and identified himself. The officer on the other end of the phone said,
"Rev, we're glad you called. We have a question to ask you, and

frankly we're all pretty embarrassed that we have to ask you this question." The pastor said, "Go ahead, ask!" The policeman said that he had driven past the church the pastor served and had read the sermon title that was being advertised on the church's outdoor sign. He needed to know whether that was the title the pastor wanted. He went on to explain that the sign read, "God is coming soon, and He is really ticked!" The pastor told the officer that wasn't his sermon title and that it should be taken down.

1. Why do you suppose the pastor had the sign taken down? What might have been an appropriate ending to the first words of the sign, "God is coming soon, and He …"?

2. If you had the responsibility of putting words on an outdoor church sign, what message would you display that would reflect an Advent message? Why?

Inform

Review the summaries of the lessons appointed for the Fourth Sunday in Advent.

2 Samuel 7:(1–7) 8–11, 16—These verses tell of David's desire to build a temple in Jerusalem to house the ark of the covenant. In consulting the prophet Nathan, David sought God's will. David in his desire to build a temple is reminded by God through Nathan of the Lord's priorities. David really reflected in his desire a pagan notion that the gods were interested in human beings only as builders and maintainers of their temples and as practitioners of their cult. Instead, the Lord has provided Israel rulers only to shepherd His flock. God's words focus David's attention not on earthly issues but instead on the everlasting kingdom for the house of David that would come through the Messiah.

Romans 16:25–27—Paul reminds the Roman Christians of Jesus Christ, who called them by the Gospel in order that He might reveal to them the riches of God's grace and mercy. Jesus Christ came to redeem all people.

Luke 1:26–38—God presents Himself to the world in an incredible way. A young woman without pedigree is chosen by Him to be the mother of the Messiah. God has chosen to have His son presented to the world as a helpless infant, born in humble circumstances. But still He is the Son of God and the Savior of the world; a Savior with whom the whole world, even the lowly and downcast, can identify.

1. How does God's Word spoken through the prophet Nathan to David indicate that at times even that which seems most noble to human beings may not be God's will?

2. How might David's seeking God's will even when all indicators point to the wisdom of his decision be important to us as we make decisions in our life? in our family? in our congregation?

3. How might God's action in bringing Jesus into this world serve as a reminder that God's plans may be very different than ours?

4. What assurance does God's working in mysterious ways provide us as things in our lives don't go as we have planned or desired?

5. How do Paul's words to the Roman Christians assure them that God has been and will continue to be active in their lives and in the world?

6. Why would God's plan continue to be a mystery if it had not been revealed by Him?

Connect

1. Think about what God has revealed to you today through His Word. What might a sign in front of your church say about the theme of the lessons for today?

2. Place yourself in the shoes of the parents of Mary and Joseph. Imagine how you would feel. What you would say each time these young people told you that Mary's pregnancy is "proof" that God is with them?

3. God's promise of a Messiah began thousands of years before the birth of Jesus. Do you believe that the fact that Jesus' birth was no "last minute" idea helped make it easier for others to believe that in Jesus and His birth God was truly present?

4. Jesus means "God saves." What does the name of Jesus tell us about the presence of God in our lives?

5. We pray in the Lord's Prayer, "Thy will be done." At times we may question God's will, particularly if it doesn't match our will. How can reviewing God's plan of salvation as revealed in Scripture enable the Holy Spirit to strengthen our faith so that in all circumstances we can pray with boldness, "Thy will be done"?

During This Week

1. Speak to a person who has just experienced difficulty in his or her life. Determine whether they believe that God was present with them throughout the experience. Share with them an experience in your life when you questioned God's presence and how God worked through that situation to draw you closer to Him.

2. Write for yourself an account of a time God made Himself present and strong for you. After you've written it, begin to prepare a manuscript of your story and memorize it if you can. This will enable you to share with others who may doubt how God came to save His people.

3. Write a letter to your grandchildren. For some of you, particularly those who have no grandchildren this will be a long stretch. Those of you who have no children should "make-believe." Write your grandchildren and tell them about how God has made Himself known in your life.

Closing Worship

Sing or speak together "Let Us Ever Walk with Jesus" (*LW* 381).

> Let us every walk with Jesus,
> Follow His example pure,
> Through a world that would deceive us
> And to sin our spirits lure.
> Onward in His footsteps treading,
> Pilgrims here, our home above,
> Full of faith and hope and love,
> Let us do our Father's bidding.
> Faithful Lord, with me abide;
> I shall follow where You guide.
>
> Let us suffer here with Jesus
> And with patience bear our cross.

Joy will follow all our sadness;
Where He is, there is no loss.
Though today we sow no laughter,
We shall reap celestial joy;
All discomforts that annoy
Shall give way to mirth hereafter.
Jesus, here I share Your woe;
Help me then Your joy to know.

Let us gladly die with Jesus.
Since by death He conquered death,
He will free us from destruction,
Give to us immortal breath.
Let us mortify all passion
That would lead us into sin;
Then by grace we all may win
Untold fruits of His creation.
Jesus, unto You I die,
There to live with You on high.

Let us also live with Jesus.
He has risen from the dead
That to life we may awaken.
Jesus, since You are our head,
We are Your own living members;
Where You live, there we shall be
In Your presence constantly,
Living there with You forever.
Jesus, let me faithful be,
Life eternal grant to me.

(Text copyright © 1978 *Lutheran Book of Worship*.)

Scripture Lessons for the Nativity of Our Lord

Read the following Scripture lessons appointed for the Nativity of
Our Lord: Isaiah 62:10–12; Titus 3:4–7; Luke 2:1–20.

Session 5

The Nativity of Our Lord

Isaiah 62:10–12; Titus 3:4–7; Luke 2:1–20

Focus

Theme: *Our Salvation Has Come*

Law/Gospel Focus

The people whom God created disobeyed Him in the Garden of Eden. From that time on people responded sinfully to God and each other. They even killed those whom God sent to lead them back to Him. In spite of people's sin, God responded to them in love and mercy by sending His only Son, Jesus, into this world to live among them, suffer and die on a cross for them, and rise victorious from the grave, proclaiming victory over sin, death, and the power of the devil for them.

Objectives

By the power of the Holy Spirit working through God's Word we will

1. affirm that Jesus is the long-awaited Messiah and Savior of the world;
2. rejoice in the wonderfully humble way that God sent His Son into the world;
3. celebrate that Jesus comes not just for those of the lost house of Israel but also for the Gentiles of the world;
4. stand in awe of God's activity in history, including His ability to use the most powerful nation on earth to serve His own desires;
5. glorify and praise God for sending our Savior.

Opening Worship

Sing or speak together stanza 1 of "Joy to the World" (*LW* 53).

Joy to the world, the Lord is come!
Let earth receive its King;
Let ev'ry heart prepare Him room
And heav'n and nature sing,
And heav'n and nature sing,
And heav'n, and heav'n and nature sing.

Then pray together,
    O God, because You once caused this holy night to shine with the brightness of true light, grant that we who have known the mystery of that light here on earth may come to the full measure of its joys in heaven; through Jesus Christ, our Lord, who lives and reigns with You and the Holy Spirit, one God, now and forever. Amen.

Introduction

An old story tells of a less-than-affable old man who lived by himself in one of the inner cities of our land. He had experienced a hard life and so had learned to be very hard and cold himself. He had little time for others and even less time for God. He had never really known love, and so the idea that God could love him so much that He would send His Son to die for him made no sense to him at all. Further, he couldn't for the life of him understand why or how God would ever want to become human and live on this trouble-filled planet.

The story continues. It seems that on one Christmas Eve the lonely man was looking out his kitchen window when he happened to see the strangest sight. A group of birds that had obviously become lost on their migration south for the winter were huddled together on the snow in his backyard. The man knew that if these birds didn't find food and warm shelter they would soon die.

Trying to save the birds' lives, the man went outside and tried to herd the birds into his open door. The birds ran from him in fear. He then tried to coax them into his house by dropping bits of food in a trail that led inside his door. The birds ate the food until they got close to the man's door, and then they ran away. Finally, the man thought that he would once again go outside and this time try to grab some of the birds; he may not be able to save them all, but perhaps he could save some. The birds were too frightened and too elusive for him to catch. In utter frustration he said to himself, "If only I could become a bird just long enough to let them know that I care about them, and just long enough to save them." At that time, the legend goes, the bell from the local church began to ring, calling worshipers to celebrate the birth of the Christ. For the first time the man understood God's reason for Christmas.

Christmas is the celebration of an event that proves that God loves His fallen world. He did become one of us so that He could save us. All praise, glory, and honor be to Him!

1. How did God fulfill what the old man desired—to become one of them?

2. What did God accomplish by sending His Son to earth?

Inform

Review the summaries of the lessons appointed for the Nativity of Our Lord.

Isaiah 62:10–12—A time of deliverance and celebration is at hand for Israel. God is coming to save and restore His people from their sin-caused exile. They are summoned to go through the gates. There is no longer reason for people to be afraid and seek shelter behind the gates and city walls. God is so proud of His people that He covers them with a sign that lets the world know that they belong to Him. God's salvation is so transforming that His people receive a new name—"the holy people," "the redeemed of the Lord."

Titus 3:4–7—After describing the trouble that people without Christ live—being foolish, disobedient, led astray, slaves to various passions and pleasures, passing our days in malice and envy, hated by men and hating one another—Paul announces that the goodness and loving-kindness of God appeared in Christ Jesus, and God chose to love us and save us through Christ. Our salvation was completely and totally accomplished, "by God" and not by ourselves. Thanks to God we are no longer doomed to live lives of confusion and futility. Instead, we will live abundant lives now and eternal lives in heaven.

Luke 2:1–20—In the fullness of time, at God's perfect time, the Savior is born. In order to bring His Son to us, God uses the plans of the greatest nation known to the world at that time to serve His own purposes. Jesus is born in Bethlehem as foretold by the prophets. He is a direct ancestor of King David. God has kept His promise to King David. Jesus is born in a lowly manner, wrapped in swaddling cloths, and laid in a manger. God brings the good news of salvation to the humble shepherds. He elevates them before the world by serenading them with a choir of His angels. God comes to save His people and does it in such a wonderful way as to let the whole world know that He is their Savior regardless of background or social setting.

1. Ancient people went through the gates of their cities only during times of peace. The birth of Christ brings peace on earth. He brings us the peace that passes all understanding. Describe the peace that Jesus brought to earth. How do you experience this peace?

2. God covers His people with a sign, a banner that identifies them as His own. How did God claim us as His people? See Titus 3:3–7.

3. Paul makes it clear God saves us—we do not save ourselves. Nowadays many people believe and teach that it doesn't matter what religion a person embraces because all religions are the same. The only thing that matters about religion is that we are sincere in our practice of the religion we have chosen. What does this passage from Titus tell us about "the just pick a religion" notion of salvation? How does this passage assure us, especially when we realize that often we fail to live up to God's expectations?

4. Angels appear whenever God's plan of salvation is being announced or executed. It is an angel that executes God's judgment on Egypt. An angel appears to Zechariah, to Mary, and to Joseph. Angels minister to Jesus after He had overcome the devil's temptations in the wilderness. Angels are present to meet those who come to Jesus' empty tomb on Easter morning. Why do you suppose angels were sent to the lowly shepherds the night Jesus was born?

5. The shepherds heard the angels tell them not to be afraid, "I bring you good news of great joy that will be for all people." What people did Jesus come for? How does this fact affect the way we relate to people?

6. When God brought the world's Savior into the world, He entrusted Him into the care of a human family. What does this say about God's attitude toward families?

7. God blessed Mary and Joseph with the Savior of the world. How does the trouble Jesus' family experienced speak to the popular notion that Christian homes should be free of trouble and heartache? How will God's continued presence in the lives of Mary, Joseph, and their family in the wake of difficult times provide you and your family comfort and hope as you experience difficulties?

1. A man who had belonged to the Lutheran church for all of his 95 years was having a conversation with his Lutheran pastor-grandson. In the middle of the conversation, the grandfather said, "I just hope that God will receive me into heaven when it is my time." How might you respond to the grandfather's statement? See Titus 3:5–7.

2. A congregation that resided in a multicultural neighborhood was hoping to begin a ministry to a nearby Asian group. The suggested plan was to involve the Asian people in the mainstream of the congregation's life rather than to begin a separate congregation that shared the same facility. One of the people of the church stood up in a voters' meeting and said that if the congregation would welcome these people into the church it would split the congregation right down the middle. Comment on this situation.

3. There are those who would suggest that our country's decision to make abortion legal means that God will no longer bless us and God can no longer use us for His purposes. The thought is that there are some decisions that God just can't use for His purposes. In light of Luke 2:1–7 comment on how God can use the decisions of persons and nations.

4. Jesus came into the life of his mother Mary and turned it upside down. Luke tells us that when astonishing things happened in Mary's life because of Jesus, she pondered those things, using

them undoubtedly for strength during the days of the crucifixion. Jesus has turned our lives upside down as well. What things has Jesus done for you that you ponder in your heart?

5. The shepherds left the manger of Jesus with great joy and told everyone what God had made known to them. How are we motivated in similar ways as we leave worship—where God through His Word and Sacraments has made His salvation know to us?

<hr>

Vision

During This Week

1. Read the front page of the newspaper. Make a mental list of all the dangerous and destructive things that go on in the world. Then remember the birth of Jesus and the angel's words to the shepherds, "Glory to God in the highest, and on earth peace to men on whom His favor rests." Write those words on a piece of paper and affix them to the newspaper. Put the newspaper somewhere where others can see it and also rejoice in the fact that in Christ God has given us victory over evil.
2. Write a letter to one of your elected officials. Tell them the story of Jesus' birth. Make sure you inform them that God uses government to bring about His ultimate ends. Let him/her know that you pray regularly for them.

Closing Worship

Read responsively the following parts of Psalm 98.

Leader: "Sing to the LORD a new song, for He has done marvelous things; His right hand and His holy arm have worked salvation for Him."

Participants: "The Lord has made His salvation known and revealed His righteousness to the nations."

Leader: "He has remembered His love and His faithfulness to the house of Israel; all the ends of the earth have seen the salvation of our God;"

Participants: "Shout for joy to the Lord, all the earth, burst into jubilant song with music."

Leader: "Make music to the Lord with the harp, with the harp and the sound of singing, with trumpets and the blast of the ram's horn—shout for joy before the Lord, the King."

Participants: "Let the sea resound, and everything in it, the world, and all who live in it."

Leader: "Let the rivers clap their hands, let the mountains sing together for joy;"

Participants: "Let them sing before the Lord, for He comes to judge the earth. He will judge the world in righteousness and the peoples with equity."

All: Glory be to the Father and to the Son and to the Holy Spirit; as it was in the beginning, is now, and will be forever. Amen.

Then sing together the last stanza of "Joy to the World" (*LW* 53).

> He rules the world with truth and grace
> And makes the nations prove
> The glories of His righteousness
> And wonders of His love,
> And wonders of His love,
> And wonders, wonders of His love.

Scripture Lessons for Next Sunday

Read in preparation for the First Sunday after Christmas Isaiah 45:22–25; Colossians 3:12–17; and Luke 2:25–40.

Session 6

First Sunday after Christmas

Isaiah 45:22–25, Colossians 3:12–17, Luke 2:25–40

Theme: *Growing Up to Be Just Like the Lord*

Law/Gospel Focus

Apart from God people are doomed to be self-centered, divisive, mean, haughty, and impatient. In Christ, who triumphed over sin, the same people can and do become selfless servants of God, living out their lives with love toward God and neighbor. The Holy Spirit strengthens people's ability to love through God's Word and Sacrament.

Objectives

By the power of the Holy Spirit working through God's Word we will

1. renew our appreciation for the sovereignty of God;
2. witness the faithfulness and devotion to God that He makes possible through faith in Jesus;
3. clothe ourselves with compassion, kindness, humility, gentleness, and patience.

Opening Worship

Leader: Praise the Lord. I will extol the Lord with all my heart in the council of the upright and in the assembly.
Participants: Great are the works of the Lord; they are pondered by all who delight in them. (Psalm 111:1–2)

Say or speak together "A Great and Mighty Wonder" (LW 51).

Refrain:
Repeat the hymn again:

"To God on high be glory
And peace on earth to men!"

A great and mighty wonder,
A full and holy cure:
The virgin bears the infant
With virgin honor pure!
Refrain

The Word becomes incarnate
And yet remains on high,
And cherubim sing anthems
To shepherds from the sky.
Refrain

While thus they sing Your Monarch,
Those bright angelic bands,
Rejoice, O vales and mountains,
And oceans, clap your hands.
Refrain

Since all He comes to ransom,
By all be He adored,
The infant born in Bethl'm,
The Savior and the Lord.
Refrain

Leader: God provided redemption for His people; He ordained His covenant forever—holy and awesome is His name.

Participants: The fear of the Lord is the beginning of wisdom; all who follow His precepts have good understanding. To Him belongs eternal praise.

All: Glory be to the Father and to the Son and to the Holy Spirit; as it was in the beginning, is now, and will be forever. Amen.

Introduction

We have all heard children say that they were going to grow up to be just like someone they admire. Sometimes that person is an athlete or a teacher. Sometimes it is an actor or actress. Other times it is a musician. As children grow older, they generally stop speaking about people they want to grow up to be like.

Once, a man in his mid-forties went up to a man in his mid-eighties and said, "When I grow up, I want to be just like you."

The man in his mid-eighties was a Christian gentleman. He was active in church, courteous and kind in all his dealing with people, and well respected by his community and church. He spoke of his faith freely and sincerely. No wonder the man in his mid-forties would want to be like him.

In Christ that is possible. Disciples of Christ know that through Word and Sacrament the Holy Spirit works to strengthen faith so that they can grow up to be more Christlike.

1. Is there anyone in your life that you would like to grow up to be like?

2. What characteristics of that person most impress you?

3. In what sense is the life of discipleship a constant confession, "Jesus, I want to be like You"?

4. What characteristics of Jesus has God provided to you? What characteristics do you still desire?

5. How is the life of a Christian either growing up in Christ or dying in sin?

═══════════════ **Inform** ═══════════════

Consider the following summaries of the lessons assigned for the First Sunday after Christmas.

Isaiah 45:22–25—The Lord sent Isaiah to bring His Word to the nation of Israel. Israel had never been a patient people. Even after watching the nation of Egypt destroyed before their very eyes, they became impatient with God their "deliverer" because there was not enough water or the right kind of food in the wilderness. When Moses went up to God on Mount Sinai in order that he might receive the Ten Commandments, Israel became impatient in his absence. They manufactured a golden calf and called it their god rather than wait patiently on the Lord. In response to Israel's impatience God has been eternally patient. Certainly, the people of Israel endured exile because of their disobedience, but God did not destroy them as a nation. He tried to rehabilitate them through their exile experience so that they would turn from their sin and once again live before Him in the Promised Land. The words of this text underscore God's patience on behalf of His people, "Turn to Me and be saved, all you ends of the earth." After all these years, after all this apostasy, God welcomes home His wayward children.

Colossians 3:12–17—When faced with trouble and temptation Christians can find direction by asking, "What would Jesus do?" His life is the personification of the Christian life. As He lives in us, and we grow in Him, our personality, touched by sin, decreases and His perfect personality increases. Because they live in Christ, the Holy Spirit enables Christians to be patient and loving, bear each other's burdens, and forgive each other, just as they have been forgiven by God.

Luke 2:25–40—Mary and Joseph are examples of the kind of faithfulness God enables His people to attain. In accordance with the law and wishes of God, Jesus was circumcised and presented in the temple. It couldn't have been an easy thing to bring an infant from Bethlehem to the temple in Jerusalem, but Mary and Joseph did it. It might have been embarrassing to offer two doves or two pigeons as sacrifice for Him. Such a sacrifice made it clear they were poor. Regardless of the difficulty—physical or emotional—they did what God asked. Simeon and Anna demonstrate the love, patience, and endurance that only God makes possible to His people. Their lives are centered in the God of their salvation. They serve and worship Him daily. Their faithfulness bears a powerful witness to God before the world.

1. What things had God done for Israel that would make it possible for her to understand that "He is God, and there is no other?" What things has He done for us that makes it possible for us to declare, "He is God and there is no other?"

2. God will save His wicked children. In order to demonstrate how serious He is about saving Israel, He does something very common in the ancient world, but not so common today. Read Isaiah 45:23 to determine what that is. Comment on God's action.

3. St. Paul instructs the church at Colosse to "clothe" themselves. What does Paul means by that? What clothing does God provide for us to put on?

4. Reread Colossians 3:16. How do these words direct us to live in relationship to one another?

5. Simeon tells the Lord that because He has seen Jesus, the Savior, he can depart this world in peace. We too have seen the Savior—revealed to us in God's Word. Why do we often sing Simeon's song of praise as part of the Divine Service immediately after we have received the Lord's Supper?

6. Luke tells us that Anna spoke about Jesus to all who were looking forward to the redemption of Jerusalem. What would she say to those who today are looking forward to their redemption? What can we say to those who long for redemption?

Connect

1. Someone once said, "Tough times don't last, tough people do." Comment on the truth and accuracy of that statement in light of Isaiah 45:24.

2. As the peace of Christ rules in our hearts, how might we react to the following situations: (a) a declining economy; (b) the prospect of a candidate who is not of your choice being elected president of the United States; (c) receiving news that two of your lifelong friends are getting a divorce; (d) your annual physical examination.

3. St. Paul exhorts us to do all things "In the name of the Lord Jesus." What percent of your life do you spend doing things in the name of the Lord? in the name of yourself? What comfort does God provide you as you confess your lack of faithfulness in speaking, thinking, or doing in Jesus' name?

4. Is there anyone in your congregation or from your Christian acquaintances who resembles Simeon or Anna? Who? How is this person's life similar to theirs?

5. What goals does Luke 2:40 set for Christian parents?

================ **Vision** ================

During This Week

1. Pay special attention this week to those who demonstrate kindness and compassion to you. Say to them, "I give thanks to God for providing you this gift."
2. Make a list of three things that you want and/or need to "turn from" in your life. Pray about them daily and develop a plan that will enable you to change. Tell someone you trust what you are trying to do so that they can support you.

Closing Worship

Sing or speak together "God of Grace and God of Glory" (*LW* 398).

> God of grace and God of glory,
> On Your people pour Your pow'r
> Crown Your ancient church's story;
> Bring its bud to glorious flow'r.
> Grant us wisdom, grant us courage
> For the facing of this hour,
> For the facing of this hour.
>
> Lo, the hosts of evil round us
> Scorn the Christ, assail His ways!
> From the fears that long have bound us
> Free our hearts to faith and praise,

Grant us wisdom, grant us courage,
For the living of these days,
For the living of these days.

Save us from weak resignation
To the evils we deplore;
Let the gift of Your salvation
Be our glory evermore.
Grant us wisdom, grant us courage,
Serving You whom we adore,
Serving You whom we adore.

Scripture Lessons for Next Sunday

Read the following Scripture lessons in preparation for the Second Sunday after Christmas: Isaiah 61:10–62:3; Ephesians 1:3–6, 15–18; John 1:1–18.

Session 7

Second Sunday after Christmas

Isaiah 61:10–62:3; Ephesians 1:3–6, 15–18; John 1:1–18

Focus

Theme: *Reflecting the Light of God*

Law/Gospel Focus

Because of sin our world was plunged into darkness, causing confusion, despair, division, and death. God in Christ entered into our place of darkness and took the darkness upon Himself. He destroyed the power of darkness on the cross. His loving and forgiving presence in our lives brings light to shine on us and through us.

Objectives

By the power of the Holy Spirit working through God's Word we will

1. understand that because of sin people live in darkness filled with sickness, crime, depression, and death;
2. recognize that God in Christ Jesus is the only true source of light and life;
3. confess Christ's power in our lives so that His light can reflect through us and into the sin-darkened world.

Opening Worship

Begin by singing the first stanza of "Joy to the World" (*LW* 53).

> Joy the world, the Lord is come!
> Let earth receive its King;
> Let every heart prepare Him room
> And heav'n and nature sing,
> And heav'n and nature sing,
> And heav'n and heav'n and nature sing.

Then speak responsively Psalm 147:12–20.

Leader: "Extol the LORD, O Jerusalem; praise your God, O Zion,"

Participants: "For He strengthens the bars of your gates and blesses your people within you."

Leader: "He grants peace to your borders and satisfies you with the finest of wheat."

Participants: "He sends His command to the earth; His word runs swiftly."

Leader: "He spreads the snow like wool and scatters the frost like ashes."

Participants: "He hurls down His hail like pebbles. Who can withstand His icy blast?"

Leader: "He sends His word and melts them; He stirs up His breezes, and the waters flow."

Participants: "He has revealed His word to Jacob, His laws and decrees to Israel."

Leader: "He has done this for no other nation; they do not know His laws. Praise the Lord."

All: Glory be to the Father and to the Son and to the Holy Spirit; as it was in the beginning, is now, and will be forever. Amen.

Then sing together stanza 4 of "Joy to the World."

He rules the world with truth and grace
And makes the nations prove
The glories of His righteousness
And wonders of His love,
And wonders of His love,
And wonders, wonders of His love.

Introduction

Robert Fulghum in his book, *It Was on Fire When I Lay down on It*, tells how he had a favorite question to ask whenever he attended a lecture or seminar and the leader would ask, "Are their any final questions?" Regardless of what the topic was he always asked the same question, "What is the meaning of life?" Sometimes the speaker would just laugh and go on, but on one occasion the speaker reached

52

into his wallet and pulled out a small piece of mirror which he displayed to the group. He went on to share how the home in which he grew up in Europe was destroyed in war. He himself had been incarcerated by the enemy. When released he went back to his home and gazed into the rubble. Everything was destroyed. As he was ready to leave the site he saw light shining from somewhere. He looked to the ground and found what appeared to be a piece, in fact the only piece, of the mirror that hung in his mother's dining room. It looked like a monument to destruction. The man took the piece with him. After a time he realized that the piece of mirror had a very positive quality. Yes, it reflected the light but because of its small size it was capable of getting into places nothing else could get into and reflecting the light into that small dark place. "This," he said, "is the meaning of life—taking things that are broken and using them to reflect light into the darkness that no one else would be able to reach."

1. How are you and I like the broken piece of mirror this man found?

2. A mirror is unable to generate its own light. Instead, it can only reflect light. How are we as Christians like the mirror?

3. When light shines in darkness, those who see it dispersing the darkness are filled with hope and joy. In what ways can God use us to bring hope and joy to people who live in darkness?

Inform

Consider the following summaries of the lessons assigned for the Second Sunday after Christmas.

Isaiah 61:10–62:3—The words of judgment, doom, and exile that have permeated the early chapters of Isaiah now give way to unbridled joy. The Lord has forgiven His wayward children. Instead of the ashes of judgment, they are now clothed by the Lord Himself in wedding finery. Instead of being ashamed of His children, God now causes His children to bring forth such great fruit that He can use them as a witness to His power before all the world. The messenger bringing this word of the Lord to Israel says he will not rest in bringing this good news to the people of God until they all know the favor they now enjoy with God and so shine forth in righteousness and joy.

Ephesians 1:3–6, 15–18—These words serve as the opening doxology of Paul's epistle to the church at Ephesus. In the doxology the apostle summarizes the history of God's activity beginning with His creation through the redemption He provides through Christ. The church then and now needs to know that it has been blessed from on high with every spiritual blessing. Regardless of how the church might look, feel, or perform, it has every gift it needs to serve God now. God's great love for the church is demonstrated by the fact that He chose us to be His own. The way He cares for His sinful, imperfect people proves His goodness and power to the world.

John 1:1–18—In this opening section of his gospel, John lets us know that Jesus of Nazareth is no mere man. Instead, He is the eternal Word of God made flesh. He is not a part of the creation as is every other human being. He instead is the Creator. Jesus said, "Let there be light" and the light came into being with the rest of creation. In addition to bringing existence to human beings, He gives life to the world. He is the one and only source of life for the world. He is also the one and only source of light for the world. His light is bold and powerful in that it shines in the darkness that people's rebellion brought into the world. The darkness cannot stop Christ's light or control it. God sends His light to shatter our darkness because He loves us. He further demonstrates His love for us in that Jesus left the glory of heaven to come and live among us in the flesh. He came among us in the flesh so that He could show us grace and truth and empower us to live lives of grace and truth.

1. Isaiah wants Israel to know that in the hands of God they can grow like vegetables in good soil. What is it about God that makes His "soil" so good for Israel and for us?

2. Israel has been saved by God, but God hasn't saved them just for their sakes. God has been merciful to Israel for the sake of all the nations. He wants all the kings of the earth to see the glory God has given to His own, so that they might also become His own children. How can we, the "New Israel of God," show forth God's love before the nations today?

3. The crown was and is the symbol of royalty. Israel is God's crown. Believers in Jesus are also the crown of God. How has God made you His crown? See also 1 Peter 2:9–10.

4. What does the apostle mean when he says we are blessed in the heavenly realms with every spiritual blessing in Christ? How and when did we receive every spiritual blessing?

5. The apostle says you were chosen in Christ before the foundation of the world. How does it make you feel to know that God chose you to be His own before He created the world?

6. God's grace according to the apostle is "glorious." What makes His grace so glorious?

7. There are those who believe that Jesus did not exist until such time as He was conceived of Mary. What does John 1:1–2 say about that teaching?

8. Although God in Christ came and lived face-to-face with people, they did not recognize Him. Why? What does that say about the power of darkness?

9. What words of comfort does John 1:12–14 provide to us who, because of sin, know that we could never live up to God's expectations, "Be perfect" (Matthew 5:48)?

===================== **Connect** =====================

1. You find yourself at the finest restaurant in the country. You've heard about this place for years and have looked forward to dining there. Finally, you are there. You present yourself to the maître d' and announce that you have a reservation. The maître d' says that he is sorry, but you aren't dressed appropriately to dine in this restaurant. Your clothes just aren't good enough. As disappointment begins to wash over you, a man behind you offers you his jacket. His jacket will allow you to eat, but he will have to leave. He is happy to do so for your sake. What would you do in this situation? Would you take the jacket and be grateful to your "savior"? Would you refuse the gift and therefore not eat in the restaurant because of your pride? Would you take the jacket, allow yourself to be seated in the restaurant, and then take the jacket off when you think no one is looking? How do these three responses to the man's offer compare to the way people respond to God's grace in Christ?

2. God chose Israel to be His own, but instead of seeing their selection as a call to thankfulness, humility, and service, Israel saw it as an occasion for self-righteousness and haughtiness. In Christ we have been declared the beloved people of God. How does His love for us motivate us to respond? What activities characterize our response?

3. If we are blessed in the heavenly realms can earthly powers confound us? In other words, does the fact that our help comes from on high make a difference in the way we stand up against our ancient enemies—sin, death, and the power of the devil?

4. Think of the things that bring us pleasure in this world. Much of what gives us pleasure is material. According to Ephesians 1:5, God receives pleasure from saving sinners. How might God's pleasure direct us as we seek pleasure?

5. We have seen the glory of God in Christ Jesus. What activities of the church enable others to see the glory of God shining through us?

During this Week

Think of yourself as that broken piece of mirror that reflects light and manages to work itself into dark places where no one else can go. Look for dark places in which to shine. Then let Christ's light shine through you. Come back next week ready to report briefly on the response of people to whom Christ's light shined through you to them.

Closing Worship

Sing or speak together the following stanzas of "Thy Strong Word Did Cleave the Darkness" (*LW* 328).

> Thy strong Word did cleave the darkness;
> At Thy speaking it was done.
> For created light we thank Thee,
> While Thine ordered seasons run.
> Alleluia, alleluia!
> Praise to Thee who light dost send!
> Alleluia, alleluia! Alleluia without end!
>
> Thy strong Word bespeaks us righteous;
> Bright with Thine own holiness,
> Glorious now, we press toward glory,
> And our lives our hopes confess.
> Alleluia, alleluia! Praise to Thee who light dost send!
> Alleluia, alleluia! Alleluia without end!
>
> Give us lips to sing Thy glory,
> Tongues Thy mercy to proclaim,
> Throats that shout the hope that fills us,
> Mouths to speak Thy holy name.
> Alleluia, alleluia! May the light which Thou dost send
> Fill our songs with alleluias, Alleluias without end!

(Text copyright © 1969 Concordia Publishing House.)

Scripture Lessons for Next Sunday

Read in preparation for The Epiphany of Our Lord Isaiah 60:1–6; Ephesians 3:2–12, Matthew 2:1–12.

The Epiphany of Our Lord

Isaiah 60:1–6; Ephesians 3:2–12; Matthew 2:1–12

Focus

Theme: *God Shines on You, God Shines on Me, God Shines on Our Neighbors Wherever They May Be*

Law/Gospel Focus

As sin divided Adam and Eve from each other so sin has divided nations and races from one another. God's love in Christ Jesus puts an end to that division. Christ died for all people. God's love for us in Christ Jesus motivates us to share His love with all people.

Objectives

By the power of the Holy Spirit working through God's Word we will

1. see that God indeed shows no partiality—He loves all His children and so has acted in love and grace to save them all;
2. affirm all people as those for whom Jesus died;
3. embrace all whom God brings into our lives so that we might share with them God's love in Christ.

Opening Worship

Sing or speak together "O Jesus, King of Glory" (*LW* 79).

> O Jesus, King of glory,
> Both David's Lord and Son!
> Your realm endures forever,
> In heaven is Your throne.
> Help that in earth's dominions,
> From pole to farthest pole,

Your reign may spread salvation
To each benighted soul.

Oh, look on me with pity
Though I am weak and poor;
Admit me to Your kingdom
To dwell there, blest and sure.
I pray, Lord, guide and keep me
Safe from my bitter foes,
From sin and death and Satan;
Free me from all my woes.

Read responsively Psalm 72:1–7:

Leader: "Endow the king with Your justice, O God, the royal son with Your righteousness."

Participants: "He will judge Your people in righteousness, Your afflicted ones with justice."

Leader: "The mountains will bring prosperity to the people, the hills the fruit of righteousness."

Participants: "He will defend the afflicted between the people and save the children of the needy; He will crush the oppressor."

Leader: "He will endure as long as the sun, as long as the moon, through all generations."

Participants: "He will be like rain falling on a mown field, like showers watering the earth."

Leader: "In His days the righteous will flourish; prosperity will abound till the moon is no more."

All: Glory be the Father and to the Son and to the Holy Spirit, as it was in the beginning is now and will be forever. Amen.

Pray together,

Father in heaven, You have made Yourself known to the world as a God of mercy and grace. In Your mercy You love all people that You have created; red, yellow, black, and white. We praise You for Your goodness and ask You to empower us so that we might make Your love known to the world in the way we love and serve the whole world. In Jesus' name, Amen.

Introduction

Talk-show host, Oprah Winfrey, did a segment of her show centering on the reuniting of families who had been separated for decades. She brought uncles and nephews, aunts and nieces, and cousins long removed from one another together. At first glance this doesn't sound like a particularly noteworthy accomplishment. But the story goes on. The unique thing about these people was that in every case the members of the family were of a different race. One uncle was black and the nephew white, the aunt was white and the niece was black. As she interviewed the people she asked them how they initially felt at the prospect of being related to someone of a different race. Many weren't comfortable with it. Some were skeptical, thinking that someone was trying to play a "not so funny trick" on them. She asked them how they overcame their original concerns. The families explained that in their initial meeting they went through family trees. The discomfort continued until they found that one father linked both sides together. Then they were able to embrace one another as family. Their long ingrained prejudices began to wane.

1. St. Paul says that "the mystery ... [that] was not made known to men in other generations" but "has now been revealed by the Spirit" is that "through the gospel the Gentiles are heirs together with Israel." How does Jesus reunite those who were estranged?

2. Through the action of God the Father—sending Jesus into this world to live, to die, and to rise—we too are able to embrace those who are different as family. How can we as individuals demonstrate the unity that is ours through Jesus? How can a Christian congregation reach out to all people—embracing others as family through God's action on their behalf?

These are brief summaries of the lessons appointed for the Epiphany of Our Lord.

Isaiah 60:1–6—Isaiah tells the Israelites that the Light—the Lord Himself—shines upon them. God penetrates the darkness of sin by His presence. People of all nations will be drawn to His Light and will praise the Lord for His goodness.

Ephesians 3:1–12—Paul prays that the Gentiles might rejoice in the favor they have found with God and rest secure in the knowledge that they too are heirs of heaven. In verses 2–12, Paul speaks of the grace that was given to him when he was appointed to be a missionary to the Gentiles. Even though the work of being an apostle places great stress on Paul and often calls him to endure pain and hardship, these hardships are overshadowed by the great privilege given to him by God to extend the love and grace of God to the Gentiles.

Matthew 2:1–12—The prophecy made so long ago by Micah has come true. The King of Israel and the Savior of the world has been born. He wasn't born in Jerusalem, the seat of all power. Instead, He was born in Bethlehem. God takes the power focus off "manmade" Jerusalem and shows the world where real power comes from, namely, His own hand. The Magi demonstrate that this Babe of Bethlehem is indeed the Savior of the whole world. God's mind is made up—He loves the world and will save the world. No power on earth, not even wily Herod the Great, will be able to stop Him from accomplishing His plan of salvation.

1. Isaiah tells us that darkness covers the earth and thick darkness covers the people. Compare that to our present day and age. What are some symptoms of the darkness that we live in?

2. Isaiah says the Lord rises upon the people of Israel and His glory appears over them. How do we, whom the glory of the Lord has risen upon, demonstrate to the world that His glory appears over us?

3. How might Isaiah 60:4 serve as a defining statement for a Christian congregation today? What can we do as a church to see to it that "All assemble?"

4. Paul announces to the church at Ephesus that he is in prison "for the sake of you Gentiles." Is he bragging? What does he convey to them about their worth?

5. What does Ephesians 3:8 tell us about St. Paul? How does his confession enable him to share God's love in Christ with people—Gentiles—often considered the least by the Jewish people?

6. Why do you think King Herod the Great was disturbed when he heard that someone was looking for the King of the Jews?

7. The Old Testament and New Testament cite several occasions when God visited people in dreams and visions in order to instruct them. Most of these individuals were Jewish. What statement is God making as He reveals His will to the Magi—Gentiles—in a vision?

1. Your congregation decides they would like to start a ministry targeted toward an ethnic group in your community. You've heard horror stories of how members of other congregations stopped attending church when people of different ethnic or racial groups began to attend. If you were the pastor what would you say to the congregation?

2. "Chief of sinners though I be." How do these words from a popular hymn mirror St. Paul's words in Ephesians 3:8? How does acknowledging yourself as the chief of sinners for whom Christ died enable you to share with other sinners the love of God in Christ Jesus?

3. The Magi came to Jesus, bowed down before Him, and gave Him gifts. How might we, to whom God has revealed His Son, Jesus, respond in similar ways?

4. Reread the theme of this lesson. How might God's shining on us enable us as individuals or as a Christian congregation to shine God's love on our neighbors?

During This Week

1. Thank and praise God for sending Jesus into this world to save all people—including you, the chief of sinners.
2. Identify a person who needs to experience God's love in Christ Jesus. Think of ways you can share Jesus' love with that person. Then let Jesus' love shine through you to that person.

Closing Worship

Allow the group to offer its prayers while standing in a circle, holding hands. Encourage them to individually offer all their special needs to the Lord. As leader, close the prayer but as you close, pray that the day will soon come when all God's people are one.

Then sing or speak together the following song.

> Jesus loves the little children,
> all the children of the world
> red and yellow black and white
> they are precious in His sight
> Jesus love the little children of the world.
>
> Jesus died for all the children
> all the children of the world,
> red and yellow black and white
> they are precious in His sight
> Jesus died for all the children of the world.
>
> Jesus rose for all the children
> all the children of the world
> red and yellow black and white
> they are precious in His sight
> Jesus rose for all the children of the world.

Scripture Lessons for Next Sunday

Read in preparation for the first Sunday after the Epiphany Isaiah 42:1–7; Acts 10:34–38; Mark 1:4–11.

Session 9

The Baptism of Our Lord

Isaiah 42:1–7; Acts 10:34–38; Mark 1:4–11

Focus

Theme: *Baptismal Power*

Law/Gospel Focus

Ever since the Fall, people have been unable to shed the ravages of sin from their lives. Jesus came among us, and through His death on the cross He saved us from sin and its ultimate result—death. Through Holy Baptism God claims us as His own and enables us by the power of the Holy Spirit to live our lives in service to Him; proclaiming through our words and actions salvation from sin that He provides to all people through Jesus.

Objectives

By the power of the Holy Spirit working through God's Word we will

1. recognize that through His baptism, Jesus humbled Himself to fulfill all that God required of sinful people;
2. believe that Baptism is more than mere water but is water connected with God's command and promise that washes us clean from our sin, makes us an heir of heaven, and gives us spiritual gifts to use to serve Him in our lives;
3. affirm the power of God at work in our lives through our Baptism to enable us to resist temptation to sin.

Opening Worship

Speak the words from Luther's Small Catechism regarding Baptism.

Leader: What is Baptism?

Participants: Baptism is not plain water, but it is the water included in God's command and combined with God's Word.

Leader: Which is that Word of God?

Participant: Christ our Lord says in the last chapter of

Matthew: "Therefore go and make disciples of all nations, baptizing them in the name of the Father and of the Son and of the Holy Spirit.

Leader: What benefits does baptism give?

Participant: It works forgiveness of sins, rescues from death and the devil, and gives eternal salvation to all who believe this, as the words and promises of God declare.

Leader: Which are these words and promises of God?

Participants: Christ our Lord, says in the last chapter of Mark: "Whoever believes and is baptized will be saved; but whoever does not believe will be condemned."

Leader: How can water do such great things?

Participants: Certainly not just water, but the word of God in and with the water does these things, along with the faith which trusts this word of God in the water. For without God's word the water is plain water and no Baptism. But with the word of God it is a Baptism, that is, a life-giving water, rich in grace, and a washing of the new birth in the Holy Spirit, as St. Paul says in Titus, chapter three: "He saves us through the washing of rebirth and renewal by the Holy Spirit, whom He poured out on us generously through Jesus Christ, our Savior, so that, having been justified by His grace, we might become heirs having the hope of eternal life. This is a trustworthy saying."

Leader: Father in heaven, we thank You for the gift of Baptism. We thank You for sending Jesus, who came to earth to fulfill all that the Law required of us. Strengthen us in our own Baptism so that we might not rest until all the world knows the blessing of this Your gift of life. Amen.

Introduction

A pastor of a large congregation asked the chairman of that congregation to deliver a speech to the whole church. The speech was delivered in order to encourage congregational members to give gifts to a building fund. The pastor knew that the young man was quite eloquent and wonderfully committed to the Lord and His church. He knew he had asked the right man to speak. The chairman walked to the podium, greeted his fellow members warmly, and began his speech by saying, "I want you to know that the most expensive thing I ever did in my life was join this church." The congregation laughed, the pastor tried to.

1. The young church leader suggested that belonging to the church costs a person something. What do you think? If it does cost us something, what does it cost?

2. What did your church membership cost Jesus?

3. In his treatise on Christian liberty, Martin Luther writes that, of all people, Christians are the most free and slave to no one. But at the same time Christians are the most bound and the most obligated. What do you think Luther meant?

4. At Jesus' baptism the Holy Spirit descended upon Him like a dove. The Bible teaches that the Holy Spirit descends upon all who are baptized. Comment on these words once spoken to a pastor: "Pastor, my husband is Lutheran but I'm not anything. Don't get me wrong, I believe in God and all, it's just that I get 'turned off' by organized religion. My husband insists on having the baby baptized, I don't really see the need for it, but if he insists, we'll have it done. I mean, what's the difference?"

Read the following summaries of the lessons appointed for this Sunday.

Isaiah 42:1–7—Isaiah opens this chapter with reference to a servant that God upholds, a chosen One in whom God delights. The word *servant* is used in the Old Testament to refer to several people, including Abraham, Moses, David, and even Cyrus, king of Persia. The nation of Israel itself is often referred to as the servant of God. The servant referred to here can be none other than our Lord Jesus. The description of the servant included here is an unmistakable description of Jesus. Jesus will bring justice to the nations, not with war, but through love.

Acts 10:34–38—In this section of the book of Acts God is preparing His people to undertake perhaps their biggest challenge—the inclusion of the Gentiles into their midst. The words from this section follow an account of Peter at the house of Cornelius. Cornelius was a Gentile. God sent Peter there through a vision. A vision prepared Cornelius for Peter's visit. Peter declares now that it is the will of the Lord that Jew and Gentile are one. Peter focuses on Jesus' ministry, beginning with His baptism. The Gentile Cornelius and his household, after hearing the Gospel, are baptized in the name of Jesus (Acts 10:48).

Mark 1:4–11—In the beginning verses of his gospel, Mark wants us to know that Jesus is the Son of God and the Savior of the world. He begins building his case for that truth by informing us that John the Baptist came to prepare Jesus way in keeping with many messianic expectations. The preparation that John calls people to is a baptism of repentance for the forgiveness of sins. John's ministry was extremely successful, so successful in fact, that it seems that there were some who thought that he might be the Christ. This explains his words to the people, "After me will come one more powerful than I, the thongs of whose sandals I am not worthy to stoop down and untie. I baptize you with water, but He will baptize you with the Holy Spirit."

This occasion marked the beginning of Christ's messianic ministry. There were several reasons for Jesus' baptism: (1) Jesus' baptism indicated that He was consecrated to God and officially approved by Him, as especially shown in the descent of the Holy Spirit and the words of the Father. (2) At Jesus' baptism, John publicly announced the arrival of the Messiah and the inception of His ministry. (3) By His baptism Jesus completely identified Himself with people's sin and failure (though He Himself needed no repentance or cleansing from sin), becoming their and our substitute. (4) His baptism was an example to His followers.

1. In Isaiah 42:1 God identifies the servant as the one He upholds and in whom He delights. Think through the life and ministry of Jesus. List the times that God upheld Him.

2. By God's grace through faith in Jesus, you are a servant of God. Think through your life and list the times that God upheld you.

3. This servant is described as gentle, yet powerful. For example, "He will not shout or cry out, or raise His voice in the streets. A bruised reed He will not break, and a smoldering wick He will not snuff out." Share examples of Christ's gentleness and power.

4. How has Jesus been gentle with us? Think of times when you acted as "a bruised reed" or a "smoldering wick."

5. In his speech Peter declares that God does not show favoritism. What does that mean for the church today?

6. What does it mean that God anointed Jesus of Nazareth with the Holy Spirit and with power? Does the fact that Jesus was "anointed" give insight into who He is?

7. Jesus did not need to be baptized. Why did He allow Himself to be baptized?

8. Peter says that Jesus went around doing good and healing all who were under the power of the devil because God was with Him. *Immanuel* means "God is with us." Since God is with us, what confidence can we have as the devil prowls about, trying to devour (tempt) us?

9. Jesus received the words from God, "You are my Son, whom I love; with You I am well pleased." Could we ever hope to have such words directed to us? See Romans 5:6–11.

Connect

1. Isaiah tells us that when God places His Spirit upon the servant, the Spirit enables the servant to bring justice to the nations. We have received the Holy Spirit. What kind of justice can we bring to the nations?

2. Isaiah 42:6 declares that God will take us by the hand and lead us, not necessarily into the places we want to go, but to the places He wants us to go. He wants us to be a light for the Gentiles. Where do you believe that that might take us today?

3. John's baptism was for repentance for the forgiveness of sins. What is the relationship between our Baptism, repentance, and forgiveness? See Acts 2:38.

4. Jesus brought the good news of peace to the world—peace that He Himself gave to the world through His death and resurrection. We were baptized into His death and resurrection. Therefore we too bring good news of peace to the world. How can you and your congregation bring the good news of peace to your community? to the world?

Vision

During This Week

1. Find out who will be the next person baptized in your congregation. Write that person or his/her parents a letter. In the letter tell the person what they can expect from their Baptism, and how your Baptism has affected your life. Encourage them in their own Baptism and life of faith.
2. Make a phone call to the children for whom you are a baptismal sponsor. Find out how they are doing in their Christian life. Present yourself as one who is praying for them and ready to help them any time they might need you.

3. Your Baptism launched you on a God-given mission of service to the world. Take time this week to think about what that mission is, and write your own personal mission statement. Keep it next to your daily devotional material, so you can refer to it and be focused daily by it.

Closing Worship

Complete the reading of Luther's explanation of Baptism.

Leader: What does such baptizing with water indicate?

Participants: It indicates that the Old Adam in us should by daily contrition and repentance be drowned and die with all sins and evil desires, and that a new man should daily emerge and arise to live before God in righteousness and purity forever.

Leader: Where is this written?

Participants: St. Paul writes in Romans, chapter six: "We were therefore buried with Him through baptism into death in order that, just as Christ was raised from the dead through the glory of the Father, we too may live a new life."

Then sing the following stanzas of "Dearest Jesus, We Are Here" (*LW* 226).

> Gracious head, Your member own;
> Shepherd take Your lamb and feed it;
> Prince of Peace, make here Your throne;
> Way of life, to heaven lead it;
> Precious Vine, let nothing sever
> From Your side this branch forever.
>
> Now into Your heart we pour
> Prayers that from our hearts proceeded.
> Our petitions heav'nward soar;
> May our fond desires be heeded!
> Write the name we now have given;
> Write it in the book of heaven!

Leader: Go in peace, serve the Lord.

Participants: Thanks be to God!

Scripture Lessons for Next Sunday

Read in preparation for the Second Sunday after the Epiphany 1 Samuel 3:1–10; 1 Corinthians 6:12–20; and John 1:43–51.

Session 10

Second Sunday after the Epiphany

1 Samuel 3:1–10; 1 Corinthians 6:12–20; John 1:43–51

Focus

Theme: *I'll Follow You Anywhere*

Law/Gospel Focus

Sin is seductive. It beckons us to follow it. If we heed the call of sin, we find ourselves in trouble, and ultimately we face eternal death. In His love, God calls us through His Word. Jesus destroyed the power of sin, death, and the devil when He died on the cross and rose victorious from the grave. In His love for us Jesus calls us to follow Him into the ways of peace and life and away from the things of death and destruction.

Objectives

By the power of the Holy Spirit working through the Word of God we will

1. affirm that the devil tries to lure us to participate in many behaviors that violate our relationship with God and jeopardize our lives;
2. confess that God prizes us despite our sinful condition, sent Jesus into this world to die for us, and calls us through the Gospel to be His own and follow Him throughout our lives;
3. rejoice in the good news that the life God calls us to live is one that brings wholeness and happiness in this life and eternal joy in the life that is to come.

Opening Worship

Read responsively the following selections from Psalm 62:1–8. Leader: "My soul finds rest in God alone; my salvation comes from Him."

Participants: "He alone is my rock and my salvation; He is my
fortress, I will never be shaken."

Leader: "How long will you assault a man? Would all of you
throw him down—this leaning wall, this tottering fence?
They fully intend to topple Him from His lofty place; they
take delight in lies. With their mouths they bless, but in their
hearts they curse."

Participants: "Find rest, O my soul, in God alone, my hope
comes from Him."

Leader: "He alone is my rock and my salvation; He is my
fortress I will not be shaken."

Participants: "My salvation and my honor depend on God, He
is my mighty rock, my refuge."

Leader: "Trust in Him at all times, O people; pour out your
hearts to Him, for God is our refuge."

All: Glory be to the Father and to the Son and to the Holy Spirit as it was in the beginning is now and will be forever. Amen.

Then say or sing together the following stanzas of "Let Us
Ever Walk with Jesus" (*LW* 381).

> Let us ever walk with Jesus,
> Follow His example pure,
> Through a world that would deceive us
> And to sin our spirits lure.
> Onward in His footsteps treading,
> Pilgrims here, our home above,
> Full of faith and hope and love,
> Let us do our Father's bidding.
> Faithful Lord, with me abide;
> I shall follow where You guide.
>
> Let us also live with Jesus.
> He has risen from the dead
> That to life we may awaken.
> Jesus, since You are our head,
> We are Your own living members;
> Where You live, there we shall be
> In Your presence constantly,
> Living there with You forever.
> Jesus, let me faithful be,
> Life eternal grant to me.

(Text copyright © 1978 *Lutheran Book of Worship*.)

Introduction

A Lutheran preschool teacher took her class into the church's sanctuary. Many of her students were not members of any church, so she was anxious to have them experience the joy of being in the house of God. She watched the children stare at the altar, the baptismal font, and the stained-glass windows. After a time she asked the children if they knew where they were. There was silence. She spied the pastor's three year old son sitting in the pew and asked him, "Timmy do you know where you are?" Tim replied, "Sure, I'm right here. Where would you like me to be?" That little boy was quite a theologian.

1. Right after Adam and Eve had sinned in the Garden of Eden, God came looking for them. God called, "Where are you?" How does God still ask the same question of us today? What kind of answers does He receive from us?

2. How do you think God would feel, if when He asked us where we were, we answered like the little boy, "I'm right here. Where would you like me to be?" What would such an answer say about our relationship with God?

3. Lots of people today have their mail sent to special post-office boxes and make sure that their phone numbers are unlisted so they can live their lives in anonymity. To what extremes will people go to try to keep God from knowing where they are?

4. Through the Gospel—the good news of Jesus' death on the cross for all sins—God continues to call to sinners. Why does God continue to call "Where are you?" to sinners. See John 3:16. What does God desire to give to sinners? See John 11:25–26.

76

Read the following summaries of the lessons appointed for the Second Sunday after the Epiphany.

1 Samuel 3:1–10—During the days of Samuel, Israel's worship life grieved God. Once again the people of Israel began to serve and worship strange and foreign gods. The apostasy of Israel even filtered its way into priestly households. The sons of Eli were evil, wicked, self-centered men. Eli himself was a man of less than strong conviction. God would not leave His people without leadership, and so He raises up Samuel to serve Him and Israel as a prophet. Samuel is confused by God's call. Even though he is sleeping near the ark of the covenant, that place from which it was believed that God spoke, he is convinced that the voice he hears is a human voice, and so he presents himself before Eli. We can't blame Samuel for not understanding that God was speaking to him. After all, the Scripture says that there was no frequent revelation of God in that day. Eli realizes that God is calling the boy and so instructs him that if he hears the voice again he is to answer, "Speak Lord, Your servant hears." Even in wicked days, God finds people who are faithful to Him, calls them to follow Him, and prepares them to serve Him.

1 Corinthians 6:12–20—In this section of the epistle Paul addresses the sexual sins of the people of Corinth. They believe that sexual indulgence is the same as satisfying hunger. For them both are natural and necessary. Sexuality for them is amoral—neither good nor bad. Paul reminds them that their bodies were not made for themselves or for their sexual pleasure. Their bodies were made for the Lord, and the Lord is committed to the care and nurture of their bodies. On the cross Jesus paid the price for our sin in order to buy us back from such "uncontrollable" desires. By God's grace through faith in Jesus, God has claimed us as His own. We now live for Him because we are members of His body—the church. In Christ Jesus people give up the mistaken right to be able to do whatever they want. Instead, they now spend their days doing what their Savior Jesus wants them to do—serve Him by their thoughts, words, and actions.

John 1:43–51—John shows us the power Jesus has to change people's lives. The only encounter Philip ever had with Jesus, as far as we know, is the one where Jesus asks Philip to follow Him. Philip, heeding the call of Jesus, then went to Nathanael. Nathanael isn't as trusting as Philip. He is skeptical. He makes fun of Jesus' background, asking, "Can anything good come out of Nazareth?" Jesus knows what Nathanael has said, and to demonstrate His power to the doubting Philip, Jesus "teases" Philip, calling him a true Israelite in whom there is nothing false. Jesus' power astonishes Nathanael. Jesus informs Nathanael that he will see much greater things than this. Early in His ministry Jesus began calling, gathering, and enlightening people unto Himself.

1. What does the fact that the word of the Lord was rare during Samuel's day tell us about the people's faithfulness during this period?

2. The Lord is calling Samuel to serve as a prophet, a charismatic leader among the nation of Israel. But Samuel is a boy. What does that tell us about whom God calls into His service and about whom God can use for His service?

3. Samuel tells the Lord that He should speak because His servant is *listening*. How is *listening* to the Lord different from *hearing* the Lord?

4. A rhyme from childhood says, "Christians don't cuss and Christians don't chew, they don't even go with girls who do!" What does 1 Corinthians 6:12 say about the innate evil that can lead people to be "mastered" by things of this world? What does Paul do in order to keep from being mastered by things?

5. The people in Corinth believed that sexual desire was a natural thing just like physical hunger. Therefore, they concluded that sexual desire could not be considered evil. What evidence is there in the world today that many people continue to embrace the Corinthians' way of thinking?

6. Jesus changes the natural concept of who owns our bodies and what our bodies are for. By His death on the cross He purchased us back from sin. We belong to Him. What would Jesus say to a person who chooses to drink too much, smoke too much, eat too much, work too much, or play too much and justifies it by saying, "After all, it is *my* body"?

7. What did Jesus mean when He told Philip and Nathanael to follow Him? What level of commitment did Jesus get? Jesus continues to call people today to "follow Me" through the Gospel. What level of commitment does Jesus desire from us whom He has called?

8. The lesson from Corinthians makes it clear that God desires those whom He has called to flee from those things that would drag us away from Him, including sexual immorality. What other things of this world might Satan use to lure us away from God and His desire for our lives—to serve Him?

9. What does God invite us to do when we fail to follow Him. See 1 John 1:9. How does God continue to strengthen our faith so that we might resist temptation and follow Him every day of our lives? For help, see 2 Timothy 3:14–17.

Connect

1. Share with a partner how Jesus called you to "follow Me."

2. Given the wickedness that exists in the world today, it might be easy to believe that we also are in a time when "the word of God is rare." How do we as Christians know that is not true?

3. Make a list of three things that the Lord desires you to do as you "follow Me." Remember, the Lord continues to strengthen faith through Word and Sacrament.

4. Make a list of three things from which you believe the Lord desires you to flee. By what means will God empower you to do that which He desires. See Psalm 119:105.

5. When God calls people, He calls them into service. God is always quick to equip people for that service. He equipped Samuel. He

80

equipped the disciples with the ability to preach the Gospel, heal the sick, and raise the dead. With what has he equipped you personally that He can use in His service?

6. You are not your own, you were bought with a price. Make a list of six things you can do to glorify God with your body.

=============== **Vision** ===============

During This Week

1. Write a letter to someone who makes a living through immoral activities. It may be the owner of an adult bookstore or the agent for the state lottery in your neighborhood. In your letter stress your disappointment in their product and let them know that you are praying that God would lead them away from such activity to a more God-pleasing life.
2. Take a health inventory. Ask yourself about your general health. Is there any problem or symptom that you have ignored that should be looked into? Is there a habit you need to break? Has your health been so good you have just taken it for granted? Maybe now is a good time to give a special gift to someone in thanksgiving to God for your health? Take whatever action is appropriate given your general state of health and know that while you do, you are praising the name of Jesus who has called you to be His own.
3. Write the words of Psalm 119:105 on small note cards. Place the cards in places where you will be reminded of God's power when you are tempted to stray.

Closing Worship

Sing or speak together the following stanzas of "May We Your Precepts, Lord, Fulfill" (*LW* 389).

May we Your precepts, Lord fulfill
And do on earth our Father's will
As angels do above;
Still walk in Christ, the living way,
With all Your children and obey
The law of Christian love.

So may we join Your name to bless,
Your grace adore, Your pow'r confess,
To flee from sin and strife.
One is our calling, one our name,
The end of all our hopes the same,
A glorious crown of life.

Spirit of life, of love and peace,
Our hearts unite, our joy increase,
Your gracious help supply.
To each of us the blessing give
In Christian fellowship to live,
In joyful hope to die.

Scripture Lessons for Next Sunday

Read in preparation for the Third Sunday after the Epiphany
Jonah 3:1–5,10; 1 Corinthians 7:29–31; Mark 1:14–20.

Session 11

Third Sunday after the Epiphany

Jonah 3:1–5, 10; 1 Corinthians 7:29–31; Mark 1:14–20

Focus

Theme: *Called by the Gospel, Enlightened with His Gifts*

Law/Gospel Focus

Although sin has made our world a "vale of tears," sin also leads us to become satisfied, complacent, and protective of our broken existence. Jesus came to this world to wipe away our tears. His love for us demonstrated by His death on the cross melts our complacency and replaces it with everlasting peace and joy.

Objectives

By the power of the Holy Spirit working through God's Word we will

1. confess our sin and the brokeness it has caused and rejoice in the forgiveness God provides through faith in Jesus;
2. understand that God calls people to faith in Christ Jesus through His Gospel;
3. witness to others Jesus' love so that they too can experience a new and abundant life filled with peace and joy;
4. affirm that the second coming of Christ is imminent and should affect the decisions we make in our lives.

Opening Worship

Speak or sing together "Amazing Grace, How Sweet the Sound" (*LW* 509).

Amazing grace! How sweet the sound

That saved a wretch like me!
I once was lost but now am found,
Was blind but now I see!

The Lord has promised good to me,
His word my hope secures;
He will my shield and portion be
As long as life endures.

Through many dangers, toils, and snares
I have already come;
His grace has brought me safe so far,
His grace will see me home.

Yes, when this flesh and heart shall fail
And mortal life shall cease,
Amazing grace shall then prevail
In heaven's joy and peace.

Introduction

A four-year-old boy used to love nothing better than sneaking into his parents' bedroom and wrapping himself in their curtains. He would roll himself up tight as fast as he could and then unroll himself as fast as he could. His parents caught him more than once. They told him that one day he would knock those curtains down and when he did he would be in real trouble. One day his father came home from work and heard the boy rolling himself up in the curtains in the bedroom. As he quickly started to the room to stop the boy, he heard a crash. The curtains had fallen on top of the boy. The father called the boy's name; the call was much more filled with concern than it was with anger. But the little boy couldn't hear the concern. All he heard was the voice of a father who promised that he would be in real trouble if ever he knocked down the curtains. In fear the little boy ran into his parent's closet and hid behind the clothes. The father looked inside the closet and saw the little boy's feet sticking out beneath the clothing. He called his name. There was no answer. He called his name again and asked him to come out. Again, there was no answer. The father could see that the fellow was shaking for fear, so he said,

"Son, come on out. Dad isn't going to spank you. I want to make sure that you are all right." At the assurance that he wouldn't be punished the little boy appeared, apologized, and promised to never do it again.

1. The little boy was warned by his parents that "on the day that he broke the curtains, he would surely … get in trouble." The warning did no good. God gave Adam and Eve a similar warning regarding the fruit of the Tree of the Knowledge of Good and Evil, and it did no good. We too have been warned of the effects of sin on our lives. Do we listen?

2. When the boy realized he was in trouble, he ran from the sound of his father's voice, even though his father had given him life and sustained that life every day. In the light of his sin, he was sure that his father would punish him, and he wanted no part of that. What motivates people to run from God today?

3. The boy hid until his father announced that he was not going to punish him. Once he knew he had nothing to fear, he came out. How is the Gospel of Jesus Christ—Jesus took the punishment for our sin when He suffered and died on the cross—like the father's words to his son?

4. Some people in our world might consider that the father who promised the son that he would not punish him was acting weak by allowing his son to get away with something. What do you think? Do you believe that is true? Did God become weak in Christ Jesus?

Read the following summaries of the lessons appointed for the Third Sunday after the Epiphany.

Jonah 3:1–5,10—Jonah was called by God to go to Nineveh and share His word. Jonah experienced the consequences of his misbehavior and wound up in the belly of a great fish. God chose to give Jonah a second chance. Jonah arrived in Nineveh and proclaimed the word of the Lord. The people of Nineveh repented from the least to the greatest, and God chose not to destroy them. God demonstrated His compassion to the people of Nineveh. The Lord's compassion for the Ninevites angered Jonah. God's commission to Jonah showed His mercy to the Ninevites. God's last words to Jonah emphatically proclaimed His concern for all people and all creatures. See Jonah 4:10–11.

1 Corinthians 7:29–31—These words come in the middle of a chapter that addresses the question of marriage and sexuality. The apostle Paul lets the church at Corinth know that because they are the redeemed children of God their concern for spiritual matters should be of ultimate importance. Nothing should get in the way of our devotion to Christ. Our devotion becomes all the more urgent when one realizes that the return of Christ is imminent. It behooves the whole church to do as Paul has done—to focus his whole life on the salvation of souls. Our concern for human things like food, shelter, clothing, and sex should decrease, because these things will not endure. They are only a part of this world and this world will pass away. Instead, Paul urges the Corinthians to devote themselves to Christ Jesus and His service.

Mark 1:14–20—John's imprisonment marks the end of an era and a mission. The era of the prophets who proclaimed the Word of God to Israel and foretold the coming of the Messiah had come to an end. John was the last of their number identified as such by his clothing and demeanor. Now in Jesus the messianic prophecies are fulfilled, and the Word of God now stands face to face with the people of God. The era of truth and grace has begun. Jesus inaugurates a reign of love. His message is much different from John's. John proclaimed a baptism of repentance for the forgiveness of sins. Jesus announced the kingdom of God is near. People who repent now hear good and glorious news of love and salvation from God. This good news and its messenger are very attractive to people who know they are dying in their sin. When Jesus calls these fishermen in love, they leave everything behind and follow Him. His love overwhelms them. Jesus doesn't just offer them personal security. Instead, He offers them meaning and purpose in life. Jesus pledges to use Simon and Andrew as fishers of men to bring salvation to the whole world. They need no time to make up their minds. The love of Christ compelled them to leave their nets and their old lives and follow Jesus.

1. Nineveh was a major city belonging to one of Israel's most feared foes, the Assyrians. During the exile, the bloodthirsty Assyrians would do such things as tie their captives together with a line. Attached to the line were fishhooks that were then pushed through the noses of the captives. Their treatment of captives was brutal. Assyrians had abused God's chosen people. What does the Lord's desire to forgive them say about His ability to love and forgive?

2. What does the fact that Jonah ran the other way when God called him say about our human nature? What does Jonah's anger toward God's compassion for the Ninevites say about people's ability to forgive?

3. The apostle Paul was absolutely sure that the Lord would return even in his own lifetime. For that reason he urges the Corinthians not to spend time in pursuits and activities tied to a world that will soon pass away. Do Paul's instructions to place energies in spiritual matters—those things eternal—still prove true for us today?

4. Many of us procrastinate. We put off until tomorrow things that we could do today. What does Jesus' message tell us about procrastination in the things of God? What is the danger of taking a wait and see attitude when people hear the Word God calling them to repent and believe?

5. If Jesus was interested in developing a base of support that would carry His message into the world, how wise did it seem to begin to gather simple fishermen into positions of vital service? Why do you suppose Jesus would choose such people to be His co-workers?

6. Nowadays a person can find a training program available for almost every area of ministry known to the church. According to Mark 1:17 who is it that prepares and enables people for service to and in the church? What then should be the focus of any training in the church?

7. When the disciples left their nets to follow Jesus, they left behind their means of support. They were trusting Jesus to provide for them. What might people say to someone who forfeits physical security to serve the Lord?

Connect

1. Many people and groups within our society have proven to be so dangerous or so corrupt, that many people have given up hope of them ever living a constructive life. Career criminals, drug traffickers, gang members, and others might fit into this category. What does the Lord's attitude toward the people of Nineveh say to us about the future of such people?

2. Almost every Christian congregation has members within it who are not very positive. They have trouble putting the best construction on things and on people. Many of us are sure that such persons will never change. How does the story of Jonah challenge this attitude?

3. We know that the Holy Spirit calls, gathers, and enlightens the whole Christian church on earth through the Gospel. What kind of enlightening would the Spirit bring to us as we study 1 Corinthians 7:29–31?

4. What good news does Jesus encourage His hearers to believe in? How would they demonstrate their belief in the Good News?

Vision

During This Week

1. Assuming that the days are short, sit down and make a list of all the things you hope to accomplish before you die. Prioritize the list, determine what should come first. Then after some thoughtful reflection, place a target date on each activity you hope to accomplish. Commit these activities and dates to your prayers.
2. Think of an individual or a group of people who you believe are beyond the grace of God. Their evil has been so great you are almost sure that there is no hope for them. Commit that person

or people into your prayers. Be assured that God in Christ can and will transform lives.

3. Begin each morning this week by repeating the message Jesus proclaimed, "The kingdom of God is near. Repent and believe the good news!" See what a difference placing such a focus on your day may have upon you.

Closing Worship

Sing or speak together the following stanzas from "How Can I Thank You Lord" (*LW* 385).

How can I thank You, Lord,
For all Your loving kindness,
That You have patiently
Endured my sinful blindness!
When dead in many sins
And trespasses I lay,
I kindled, holy God,
Your anger ev'ry day.

It is Your work alone
That I am now converted;
Against the sin in me
You have the power asserted.
Your mercy and Your grace,
Which rise afresh each morn,
Have turned my stony heart
Into a heart newborn.

Grant that Your Spirit's help
To me be always given
Lest I should fall again
And lose the way to heaven.
Grant that He give me strength
Against infirmity;
May He renew my heart
To serve You willingly.

Scripture Lessons for Next Sunday

Read in preparation for the Fourth Sunday after the Epiphany Deuteronomy 18:15–20; 1 Corinthians 8:1–13; and Mark 1:21–28.

Session 12

Fourth Sunday after the Epiphany

Deuteronomy 18:15–20; 1 Corinthians 8:1–13; Mark 1:21–28

Focus

Theme: *Authority and Responsibility*

Law/Gospel Focus

Eve decided to eat from the fruit of the Tree of the Knowledge of Good and Evil because she thought it would allow her to "be like God." Ever since that time people tainted by sin have struggled and fought for power and authority; often used for selfish ambition. Jesus into whose hands all authority has been given in heaven and on earth, uses His authority and power to show love toward the fallen human race. He empowers His own to use His authority in love and with responsibility.

Objectives

By the power of the Holy Spirit working through God's Word we will

1. see that God gives authority to His people on earth to speak His Word and to serve Him and others;
2. recognize that some people misuse authority by trying to gain personally from it;
3. be empowered to give up certain freedoms in order to further the cause of Christ in our world;
4. rejoice that the Gospel of Christ is so powerful that it can heal and restore people who have suffered from the effects of sin.

Opening Worship

Sing or speak together "Take My Life, O Lord, Renew" (*LW* 404).

Take my life, O Lord, renew,
Consecrate my heart to You;
Take my moments and my days;
Let them sing Your ceaseless praise.

Take my hands and let them do
Works that show my love for You;
Take my feet and lead their way,
And never let them go astray.

Make my will Your holy shrine,
It shall be no longer mine.
Take my heart, it is Your own;
It shall be Your royal throne.

Take my love; my Lord, I pour
At Your feet its treasure store;
Take my self, Lord, let me be
Yours alone eternally.

Introduction

A young pastor spent a summer Saturday afternoon cutting his lawn. It was a hot day, and the pastor became very thirsty. He decided he would like to drink some beer to quench his thirst. Dressed in blue jeans and a T-shirt he headed for the local grocery store. He picked up a six-pack of beer and took it to the express checkout line. As he waited patiently in line a lady came up behind him and asked, "Are you Pastor David from the Lutheran church?" The pastor said, "Yes." The woman then responded, "Then how do you dare buy this beer? You are leading people astray. Drunkards won't enter the kingdom of God. You may be leading people into sin. Show me in the Scriptures where the Lord directs us to buy alcohol!" The pastor, embarrassed by the commotion the woman caused, simply asked the woman if his buying beer was really that upsetting to her. She said that it was. The pastor said fine. He then took the beer back to the cooler, replaced it, and bought a six-pack of cola. The woman didn't say another word. She just left.

1. Was it wrong for the pastor to buy beer?

2. Did the pastor show weakness or strength by taking the beer back to the cooler? Why?

Inform

Review the brief summaries of the Scripture lessons for the Fourth Sunday after the Epiphany.

Deuteronomy 18:15–20—In this section of the book of Deuteronomy the people of Israel receive instruction regarding the spiritual leaders who have been given authority over them. In Deuteronomy 18:14 we learn how different the spiritual leaders of Israel are to be from the leaders of the pagans who live in the land that Israel will possess. Those leaders practice witchcraft in order to determine the will of God. It must not be so among the people of Israel. They will never need to go through meaningless contortions in order to seek the will of God. God will make sure that His people always know His will because He will raise up for them prophets, that is, people who will speak God's Word to the people as He directs them. Israel is to listen to the prophet and obey just as surely as they would if God spoke to them personally. God has put such authority upon the shoulders of the prophet that if anyone would presume to speak for God without God's authorization he should be put to death.

1 Corinthians 8:1–13—Pagan sacrifices in the first century A.D. became a problem for Christians because only part of the sacrificial animal was offered up to the deity. The remainder of the meat was sold by the priests in the local meat markets. Some Christians took issue with the idea of eating meat that had been contaminated through its contact with false gods and meaningless rituals. Corinth was filled with so-called "men of knowledge" who believed that their knowledge set them free from some traditions and rules. They would launch full ahead and eat this meat without regard for the feelings and sensibilities of weaker Christians. Paul speaks to these men of knowledge and tells them that knowledge in and of itself is nothing to be

celebrated. He states that a much higher gift is love. Love "builds up," while knowledge simply "puffs up." Paul certainly knows that there are no such things as other gods and so the meat offered to them is not unclean. It can be eaten without doing harm to a person. However, Paul is also aware that if this "harmless" activity causes a weaker brother to have a troubled conscience or a compromised faith, then even if it is his right to eat this meat, he won't do it. He loves his Christian brother and cares about his spiritual well-being.

Mark 1:21–28—This is the beginning of our Lord's ministry. He is teaching in the Capernaum synagogue. His teaching amazes the people who listen to Him because He teaches as someone who had authority unlike the teachers of the Law they had become used to. As He teaches, He is confronted by a demon who had possessed a man in the synagogue. The demon knows Him by name and begins to harass Him. Jesus demonstrates the authority He possesses by telling the demon to be quiet and come out of the man. The demon immediately obeyed. Jesus used His great power and authority to set people free from their sin and from their infirmities. In so doing He caught the attention of all who saw what He did and heard what He said. They didn't keep this news to themselves. Word about Jesus spread throughout the whole region of Galilee.

1. Why do you think God makes His directions concerning the prophets so clear to the people of Israel?

2. Nowadays people who need an advocate for themselves can give to someone they trust their power of attorney. A power of attorney allows one person to speak for another as though that person was speaking for himself or herself. In Israel the prophet spoke with "the power of attorney" for God. What would happen to the prophet who did not take his responsibility seriously? What would happen to the people who did not take the prophet seriously?

3. If the prophet spoke for God and spoke the truth of God why do you think he was generally unpopular?

4. God continues to provide His people today the authority to share His Word of Law and Gospel to people. How is God's message to sinners received?

5. The "men of knowledge" who belonged to the church of Corinth were very proud of their "accomplishment." How do you suppose they responded to Paul's words, "We know that we all possess knowledge?"

6. St. Paul encourages the Corinthians to see God as the one who possesses all knowledge (1 Corinthians 8:3). This being the case then, what do the "men of knowledge" have to be puffed up about?

7. How do the people of God use the knowledge that they have received from God? Compare that to how the "men of knowledge" used their knowledge.

8. What issues exist in today's church that may be compared to the problem St. Paul faced with weaker brothers who were being offended by Christians who ate meat offered to idols?

9. If Paul never did eat meat again, do you think he would have resented it or celebrated it? Put yourself in the same place. Would you resent or celebrate giving up some of your Christian freedom so that a weaker brother of sister would not be offended?

10. Jesus teaches as one with authority because He possesses all authority. For whom does He use this authority? For whom did Jesus ultimately give, up or put aside, His authority in order to fulfill His responsibility? See Matthew 27:45–54.

=================================== **Connect** ===================================

1. Just as Jesus exercises control over demons, His power is available to gain control over all besetting sins and destructive human inclinations. How important is it for Jesus' power to gain and maintain control over those forces in our lives?

2. The church of Jesus Christ is powerful—it is the very body of Jesus Christ. As the church confronts evil in our day and age, how are we to dispense this power?

3. In light of our study of 1 Corinthians 8:1–13, how are we to exercise our Christian freedom?

4. Compare Paul's message in 1 Corinthians 8:1–13 to 1 Corinthians 9:19–23. How do these passages speak to the following statements?
   "We've never done it that way before."
   "If they want to join us, they'll have to learn to appreciate those things that are important and meaningful to us."
   "They are different than us!"

5. How might our church continue to "become all things to all men so that by all possible means I might save some" without giving up that which is essential—to proclaim the Gospel in its truth and purity?

6. What authority and responsibility does God grant to His church today?

══════════════ Vision ══════════════

During This Week

1. Actively look for an opportunity to surrender one of your freedoms for the well-being of someone else.
2. God continues to select and to call men into the office of the holy ministry, providing them the authority and responsibility to proclaim His Law and Gospel. This week pray daily for your pastor, asking God to continue to strengthen him for service. Give thanks to God for calling your pastor to serve Him in your midst. Write

a note of thanks to your pastor for carrying out his responsibilities wisely, using the authority given to him by God.

Closing Worship

Sing or speak together "Lord Jesus, Think on Me" (*LW* 231).

> Lord Jesus, think on me
> And purge away my sin;
> From selfish passions set me free
> And make me pure within.
>
> Lord Jesus, think on me,
> By anxious thoughts oppressed;
> Let me Your loving servant be
> And taste Your promised rest.
>
> Lord Jesus, think on me,
> Nor let me go astray;
> Through darkness and perplexity
> Point out Your chosen way.
>
> Lord Jesus, think on me
> That, when the flood is past,
> I may th' eternal brightness see
> And share Your joy at last.

Scripture Lessons for Next Sunday

Read in preparation for the Fifth Sunday after the Epiphany Job 7:1–7; 1 Corinthians 9:16–23; Mark 1:29–39.

Session 13

Fifth Sunday after the Epiphany

Job 7:1–7; 1 Corinthians 9:16–23; Mark 1:29–39

Focus

Theme: *Accommodators for Christ*

Law/Gospel Focus

Our sinful nature causes us to isolate ourselves from those who are different from us. Divisions exist everywhere. Christ's death and resurrection has removed all divisions and now enables us to reach out with His love to people who come from different backgrounds and conditions.

Objectives

By the power of the Holy Spirit working through the Word of God we will

1. see that this world is indeed a veil of tears filled with anxiety, fueled by futility, and topped off by fatigue;
2. celebrate that God did not leave us in our natural state of vulnerability and depravity. Instead, He sent Jesus into the world to triumph over sin and to deliver us from disease, darkness, and death;
3. realize that because of Jesus' deliverance from the devil's domain we are compelled to share the good news of Jesus Christ with others;
4. commit ourselves to sharing the Gospel with the whole world by becoming "all things to all men so that by all possible means I might save some."

Opening Worship

Read responsively Psalm 147:1–7, 11–13.
Leader: "Praise the Lord. How good it is to sing praises to our God, how pleasant and fitting to praise Him!"

Participants: "The Lord builds up Jerusalem; He gathers the exiles of Israel."

Leader: "He heals the brokenhearted and binds up their wounds."

Participants: "He determines the number of the stars and calls them each by name."

Leader: "Great is our Lord and mighty in power; His understanding has no limit."

Participants: "The Lord sustains the humble but casts the wicked to the ground."

Leader: "Sing to the Lord with thanksgiving; make music to our God on the harp."

Then sing or speak together the following stanzas of "Praise to the Lord the Almighty" (*LW* 444).

Praise to the Lord, the Almighty, the King of creation!
O my soul, praise Him, for He is your health and salvation!
Let all who hear Now to His temple draw near,
Joining in glad adoration!

Praise to the Lord, who will prosper your work and defend
you; Surely His goodness and mercy shall daily attend you.
Ponder anew what the Almighty can do
As with His love He befriends you.

Praise to the Lord! Oh, let all that is in me adore Him!
All that hath life and breath, come now with praises before
Him! Let the amen Sound from His people again.
Gladly forever adore Him!

Leader: "The Lord delights in those who fear Him, who put their hope in His unfailing love."

Participants: "Extol the Lord, O Jerusalem; praise Your God, O Zion, for He strengthens the bars of your gates and blesses your people within you."

All: Glory be to the Father and to the Son and to the Holy Ghost as it was in the beginning is now, and will be forever. Amen.

Introduction

Eddie Jones is a professional basketball player. He plays for the Los Angeles Lakers. Eddie Jones had a difficult life growing up. He was from a broken home, and he claims that there weren't a lot of people who were there for him while he was growing up. Now that he is a professional basketball player and earning a good salary, he has involved himself heavily in charitable work within the inner city of Los Angeles. He tries to impress on minority students the importance of securing an education, working hard, and setting goals for yourself. In order to give young people a chance to taste and see how good life can be, he treats 15 young people a night to a Laker home game. He pays for the game, their food, and the souvenirs that the young people may desire. He teaches hard work, obeying the law, staying off drugs, and setting goals for yourself. He backs up his teaching with acts of love.

1. Eddie Jones realizes that if people stay within the framework of poverty the probability is great that their lives will be filled with want, anger, crime, drugs, illness, and premature death. How does this perception of life compare to Job's analysis of man's life?

2. At Thanksgiving Eddie Jones loads a van with groceries for Thanksgiving dinners. He drives the groceries into the worst neighborhoods in Los Angeles and delivers them to needy people. Sometimes he doesn't finish until late at night. People have asked him if he is afraid in such neighborhoods. He has responded by saying, "No, these neighborhoods aren't anything compared to the neighborhood I grew up in." How might Jones' attitude compare to Jesus' willingness to come into our world of tears and fears?

3. Before the beginning of the 1995 National College Athletic Association Football season, the association's rules committee determined that a team could be penalized if "excessive celebration or demonstration" took place after a touchdown. One of the actions determined to be excessive was a player dropping to one knee and praying after making a touchdown. It didn't take long

for the NCAA to learn that penalty or not, young Christian men would not stop thanking God for His protection. After less than one month, the NCAA backed down and once again players could pray without fear of penalty. Which verse of 1 Corinthians 9:16–23 compares to this activity by the players?

4. Historians who have studied the mission strategy of the Franciscan priests who established missions up and down the California coast note that before the Franciscan fathers would preach the Gospel to the Indians, they made them learn Spanish. The Indians were expected to learn Spanish, but the priests weren't expected to learn the Indian tongue. What is wrong with that mission strategy?

5. The city of Mission Viejo, California, published a bumper sticker that said, "Mission Viejo, Where Life Is Good." In addition to schools, churches, golf courses, and shopping malls Mission Viejo also has a police station with a jail, a huge multiservice hospital, two mortuaries, and a cemetery. Given these features, is the bumper sticker telling the complete truth?

6. What doors can be opened for sharing the Good News of Jesus by acts of community service, such as those done by Eddie Jones?

Review the following summaries of the three lessons appointed for the Fifth Sunday after the Epiphany.

Job 7:1–7—In this section of the book of Job, Job laments the human condition. He has already lost his family and his fortune. He is watching his health slip away. His wife's support is waning, and his friend's support is shallow. He knows he is not alone in his trouble, and so he postulates that everyone's experience in life is hard, without reward or meaning. Job is convinced that all of life is futile. Life is so short that no one will ever know we were here. No enduring mark will be made by us on the world. He is sure he will never see happiness again.

1 Corinthians 9:16 23   St. Paul knows how marvelous life in Christ Jesus is. He was lost, so lost that he was persecuting the church of Jesus Christ. Out of His great love and grace God saved Paul from a life of futility and destruction. Paul, rejoicing in his salvation and determined to share the love of Christ with the world, declares how the love of God has transformed him. He knows that in Christ Jesus he is completely free and a slave to no one. Yet at the same time, because he owes his life to Christ, he is a slave to everyone. The purpose of his slavery is not self-flagellation but instead a desire to serve others in Jesus' name. Therefore he is not too proud to share the condition of those he longs to serve and to save. If they are Jews, he behaves like a Jew in order to earn a right to have their ear. If they are under the Law, he too behaves as one under the law so that he might speak to them clearly and on their level. This passion for sharing the Gospel and for the lost is not just a passing phase in Paul's life, it is the very stuff of his life. It should be the very stuff of every Christian life.

Mark 1:29–39—Jesus has just driven out evil Spirits, He has displayed His power in a magnificent way. Yet He humbles Himself by entering the simple home of Simon and Andrew. Once there He doesn't expect to be served, instead He accommodates Himself to the situation that exists. He finds that Peter's mother-in-law is ill. He reaches out and touches her hand; an unusual occurrence in Jewish culture because the general thought was that touching an ill person immediately transferred the illness to the well person. Jesus has no fear, He, if you will, is willing to become the ill person, in order to make Peter's mother-in-law well. To show His incredible love for those who are ill, Jesus heals these folks on the Sabbath. He is much more concerned about caring for people than He is concerned about Sabbath rules. To show His love, Jesus receives all the sick and demon-possessed and heals them. He then travels throughout Galilee, healing people and casting out demons.

1. Try to imagine for a moment that you have never heard of Jesus, nor have you been exposed to the good news that the world is in the hands of a loving God. Then speculate how you would deal with the death of your children, the loss of your business and income, the loss of the respect of your spouse, and the sudden loss of your health. Write down what your thoughts and feelings might be. Then compare what you have written with what Job wrote in Job 7:1–7.

2. What is the Christian's response to Job's lament, "My days are swifter than a weaver's shuttle, and they come to an end without hope?"

3. Many people in life speak Job's sentiments in verse 7 when he says, "My eyes will never again see happiness." Is there a tragedy that a person can face that is so large that they will never again know happiness?

4. If someone tried to thank Paul for going above and beyond the call of duty in his ministry, what would Paul most likely say to them? Consult 1 Corinthians 9:15–16.

5. Those who study growing churches say that every Christian congregation and every Christian person should have a mission statement. From what St. Paul says in verse 19 what would you say his mission statement is? Would that be a reasonable mission statement for us today?

6. St. Paul says, "I have become all things to all men so that by all possible means I might save some." Does this statement indicate that Paul has absolutely no standards or principles by which he lives? Is he wishy-washy in order to win the appreciation of other people?

7. Paul trains hard to run his race. Many runners run so that they might bring glory to themselves. For whom does St. Paul run? For whom do Christians run?

8. After she was healed, Peter's mother-in-law immediately rose and served Jesus. Why did she serve Him? Was it just expected of her or was she offering her thanks to Jesus? What lesson does she teach to those of us whom Jesus saved from sin, death, and the power of the devil?

9. After a long day and night of ministry, Jesus rose early the next morning and went to a quiet place to pray. If we are to be ready to share Jesus' love with others, why do we need to spend quiet time with Him? What happens during that quiet time?

1. Think back to a time in your life when Job 7:1–7 was an accurate expression of how you were feeling. At that time, did you believe you would ever be happy again? What happened to make you happy again? How did you respond to God's work in your life?

2. Paraphrase the following words of St. Paul so that they reflect a present-day understanding of Paul's position, "To the Jews I became like a Jew, to win the Jews. To those under the law I became like one under the law to win those under the law. ... To those not having the law I became like one not having the law ... so as to win those not having the law. To the weak I became weak, to win the weak. I have become all things to all men so that by all possible means I might save some."

3. When athletes go into training nowadays, they stick to a strict diet, they conform to a rigorous practice schedule, they lift weights, and they continually review and evaluate new equipment developed that might improve their performance. What steps does "Christian discipleship training" take? See 2 Timothy 3:15–17.

4. Jesus obviously healed people on the Sabbath. This was against Jewish law. Why did He believe that this was the right and righteous thing to do? What opportunities do we have to "heal people on the Sabbath," that is, to do things for people even though what we do may not conform to tradition or to popular expectation?

During This Week

1. Christ has given us the victory over futility. Our lives can and do count for something. With that in mind, rewrite Job 7:1–7 so that it reflects the joy and peace that is ours in Christ. Bring it to class next week so that you can share it.
2. Identify those under the Law and those that are weak. Work hard on identifying with those people so that God can provide you opportunities to share Jesus with them.
3. Make a list of evil forces and influences that plague our church and world. Pray that the Lord would rid us of these.

Closing Worship

Think about people in your community who are different from you and who need to hear this Gospel. This may include caucasian people, black people, Asian people, incarcerated people, gay people, etc. Pray together now and privately throughout the week that the Lord send ministers to them who can lift up the name of Jesus before their eyes and by the Spirit's power bring them to salvation.

Scripture Lessons for Next Sunday

Read in preparation for the Sixth Sunday after the Epiphany 2 Kings 5:1–14; 1 Corinthians 9:24–27; Mark 1:40–43.

Session 14

Sixth Sunday after the Epiphany

2 Kings 5:1–14; 1 Corinthians 9:24–27; Mark 1:40–45

Focus

Theme: *Healed to Be Whole*

Law/Gospel Focus

A result of sin in this world is disease, sickness, and ultimately death. No one is immune from the results of sin, not even great military men. But God in Christ enters our world to heal us from the ravages of sin and gives us life—abundant life on earth and eternal life with Him in heaven.

Objectives

By the power of the Holy Spirit working through the Word of God we will

1. see that disease and illness is no respecter of class or status and that we are all susceptible to the results of sin;
2. celebrate the power of God that through Christ heals us of our sin;
3. recognize that our task and privilege in life is to run hard as though in a race. The race is run not for us but for others. We run so that others may know the victory of salvation that is theirs by God's grace through faith in Jesus;
4. know that God provides strength to His people as He empowers us and heals us so that we can serve Him all our days.

Opening Worship

Read responsively Psalm 32.

Leader: "Blessed is he whose transgressions are forgiven, whose sins are covered."

108

Participants: "Blessed is the man whose sin the Lord does not count against him and in whose spirit is no deceit."

Leader: "When I kept silent, my bones wasted away through my groaning all day long."

Participant: "For day and night Your hand was heavy upon me; my strength was sapped as in the heat of summer."

Leader: "Then I acknowledge my sin to You and did not cover up my iniquity."

Participants: "I said, 'I will confess my transgressions to the Lord'—and You forgave the guilt of my sin."

Leader: "Therefore let everyone who is godly pray to You while You may be found; surely when the mighty waters rise, they will not reach him."

Participants: "You are my hiding place. You will protect me from trouble and surround me with songs of deliverance."

Leader: "I will instruct you and teach you in the way you should go; I will counsel you and watch over you."

Participants: "Do not be like the horse or the mule which have no understanding but must be controlled by bit and bridle or they will not come to You."

Leader: "Many are the woes of the wicked, but the LORD's unfailing love surrounds the man who trusts in Him."

Participants: "Rejoice in the LORD and be glad, you righteous; sing, all you who are upright in heart!"

All: "Glory be to the Father and to the Son and to the Holy Spirit; as it was in the beginning is now, and will be forever. Amen."

Introduction

A young man began to experience severe abdominal pain. His physician hospitalized him and ordered a battery of tests. During his barrage of tests he found himself in a bed next to an elderly gentleman. The young man determined that the older gentleman was a nice enough guy, but he couldn't understand why this old fellow was getting so much attention. Friends, family members, and pastors kept coming in to visit this man. Once, when finally there was a moment of silence the young man asked the older man why he was in the hospital. The older gentlemen calmly said, "I have abdominal cancer, and probably not long to live." The young man was stunned. He became further amazed as days went on. Instead of lamenting and complaining, the older gentleman was in good spirits. Far better spirits than the young man who considered all this time spent in the hospital a horrible inconvenience. The young man received few visitors, and was not in a very positive mood. When his physicians would come to speak with him, he was always surly if not downright mean. He was a troubled young man. It was determined that he had an ulcer that was treatable. He could get well easily if he just followed the doctor's orders. The young man went home still unhappy. The older man went home to heaven happy.

1. Which of these two men was the sickest? Why?

2. Comment on the following assessment of the situation: "One of the men was well, but the other one was whole." Which one was which? What does that tell us about the quality of life God offers to Christians?

3. Is it possible for a person to be both healthy and whole? Share the names of people you know who are both healthy and whole. Think about people who are just healthy. Think about people who are just whole.

4. How does Jesus make us whole?

5. Nowadays everyone is interested in staying healthy. Does that necessarily mean that people then are also whole? If not, what can people do to become whole?

Inform

The paragraphs that follow summarize the lessons for the Sixth Sunday after the Epiphany.

2 Kings 5:1–14—The account of the cure of Naaman takes a dominant role in this portion of 2 Kings. We see how God uses simple people in powerful ways to accomplish His purpose. A young maid captured by the Syrians in a raid and carried into slavery is responsible for sending Naaman to Elisha so he can be healed. Naaman's arrival in Israel is not a source of joy for the king of Israel. He is sure that this is a deliberate attempt to get him into trouble with the king of Syria. The purpose of the visit arranged by God is to demonstrate that there is a prophet of God in the land. Naaman is offended by the greeting he receives from Elisha. Elisha honors God and no one else, certainly not a man. Instead of greeting Naaman in an extraordinary way or prescribing some sort of special ritual that would elevate the importance of Naaman in his own eyes and in the eyes of others, Elisha simply tells him to wash unceremoniously in the Jordan River seven times. Naaman is upset. Naaman is told that he can be healed by washing in the murky Jordan instead of washing in the crystal clear rivers of Syria. Naaman is healed. Naaman is also humbled. In short Naaman isn't just healthy, God makes him whole. Naaman returns home, worshiping the God who healed him.

1 Corinthians 9:24–27—St. Paul here tries to explain to the people of Corinth why he has spent so much energy preaching the Gospel. He uses the imagery of a runner in a race. He says that in a race all the runners run but only one wins. Just running in the race will never be enough for Paul. He has to win. He has to win because he knows that the success or failure of his performance does not affect him, but instead affects the salvation of the world. He runs hard to win the prize—souls in heaven. He also encourages Corinthians to understand that they have a responsibility to the God who saved them to run the race and run it hard. Their running hard by sharing God's love with others is a way of bringing thanks to God for His saving love in their lives.

Mark 1:40–45—The healing of the leper by Jesus stands in rich contrast with the healing of Naaman by Elisha. Naaman is told by someone he never sees to go and wash in the river. Jesus sees this leper face-to-face and touches him in order to heal him. According to Jewish law, a person who touches a leper is himself rendered unclean. He cannot stay within the company of healthy people until he can demonstrate that he doesn't have the disease himself. But Jesus is unafraid. He personally lays His hands on the infected man, and he is made whole. The healing of the leper brings good news to every person who has trouble in their lives. The good news is that Jesus has compassion on those who are unclean. Most of the world has no patience or compassion for those who find themselves sick or in trouble. Jesus takes the time to heal people in such a way as to lift them up. Again, Jesus doesn't just make people well, He makes them whole.

1. Naaman and the King of Aram were powerful men, men who would determine their own destiny. Yet when Naaman acquires leprosy he jumps at the suggestions of a simple, captured maiden from Israel. Had he stood on his laurels and rejected her humble words, he would not have received healing. What does this tell us about what it takes to be whole?

2. Naaman almost died of pride. He is incensed by the common treatment he receives from Elisha. So "offended" is he that he almost doesn't go to the Jordan to bathe. How many of us today make selfishness a symptom of our sin sickness? When has selfishness got in the way of your being whole?

3. Paul, in using the image of the race tells us that he trains with a purpose. He doesn't run aimlessly like a fellow who is just beating the air with his fists. He makes sure that everything he does in his life serves his ultimate goal—to share with others the gift of eternal life he received by God's grace through faith in Jesus.

How do we as Christians sometimes run like men who pummel the air aimlessly? How might we, as our faith is strengthened through Word and Sacrament, run the race to get the prize?

4. The leper that meets Jesus knows that Jesus has the power to make him well. His one question is whether Jesus is willing to make him well. Do people today wonder whether God is willing to heal them, keep them, and make them whole? Why?

5. Mark doesn't just tell us that Jesus healed the man with leprosy. He tells us that Jesus healed the man of his leprosy "immediately." What do you think is the significance of the word immediately?

6. Jesus desires to make all people whole. Filled with compassion, Jesus lived a perfect life and died a horrible death in our place. Jesus suffered and died on the cross to heal us from sin and give us life. In what way does He continue to reach out and touch us with His healing today?

Connect

1. Naaman is cured when he washes seven times in the Jordan River. Would the story have been any less powerful if Naaman had come to believe in the God of Israel through his involvement with Elisha and then died from leprosy?

2. Elisha and Naaman are the ones who get the greatest notoriety in the story. What would have happened had the maiden from Israel not been taken to Aram? What does this teach us about what God can do with trouble, tragedy, and people who don't appear to be powerful?

3. Naaman is disappointed that he is to be healed in such a simple, even mundane way. How does the healing of Naaman in the Jordan compare to the Sacrament of Baptism? How do people in our world also question whether or not Baptism is the proper means to salvation? Why do you suppose this is true?

4. In life everyone runs. Some run for fame, some run for fortune, some run for God. Compare and contrast the lives of such runners as John Lennon, Elvis Presley, Billy Graham, Elizabeth Taylor, and Mother Teresa.

5. Jesus came to a man who was an outcast. Lepers were the biggest outcasts in the first century A.D. Jesus breaks through all those barriers and touches the man. Who are the lepers today? Would Jesus still break through the barriers and touch them? What does this tell us of the attitude Jesus desires of His disciples?

6. Jesus became instantly popular because of His healings. He was so popular He had to stay outside towns and cities because of the

commotion He would cause. Do you think the people who would flock around Jesus were there to serve Him or to be served by Him? Does the Christian church today exist to serve Jesus or to be served by Him?

══════════ **Vision** ══════════

During This Week

1. Find someone in your life who is considered an outcast. Make it your business to see this outcast, befriend him or her, and share with him or her the Gospel.

2. Think about the race you are running for the Lord. How is your training coming? Are there things you could work on? Are you too impatient? Too opinionated? Too lethargic? Determine what change in your life would make you a better disciple and begin with the power of the Holy Spirit working through God's Word and Sacrament to make that change this week.

Closing Worship

Sing or speak together "God Loved the World So That He Gave" (*LW* 352).

> God loved the world so that He gave
> His only Son the lost to save
> That all who would in Him believe
> Should everlasting life receive.
>
> Christ Jesus is the ground of faith,
> Who was made flesh and suffered death;
> All who confide in Christ alone
> Are built on this chief cornerstone.
>
> If you are sick, if death is near,
> This truth your troubled heart can cheer:
> Christ Jesus saves your soul from death;
> That is the firmest ground of faith.

Be of good cheer, for God's own Son
Forgives all sins which you have done;
You're justified by Jesus' blood;
Baptized you have the highest good.

Scripture Lessons for Next Sunday

Read in preparation for the Seventh Sunday after the Epiphany Isaiah 43:18–25; 2 Corinthians 1:18–22; Mark 2:1–12.

Session 15

Seventh Sunday
after the Epiphany

Isaiah 43:18–25; 2 Corinthians 1:18–22; Mark 2:1–12

Focus

Theme: *A Cure for Sin!*

Law/Gospel Focus

"The wages of sin is death." Death is the ultimate consequence of the dreaded disease, sin, that infects all people. God comes to us and curses death through the death and resurrection of Jesus Christ. By God's grace through faith Jesus' victory over death is our victory over death. His love for us causes us to praise God with words and actions that proclaim His cure for sin and its deadly consequence.

Objectives

By the power of the Holy Spirit working through the Word of God we will

1. see that our sins and sinful condition bring about the evil that we must face in life, including the greatest evil—death;
2. celebrate the fact that God in Christ Jesus has forgiven our sins and provides us eternal life;
3. live our lives confidently knowing that God will speak not a no but rather a yes to us in all our needs because He loves us in Christ.

Opening Worship

Pray together:

Dear Lord Jesus, we know that You are the Holy One of God, sent for the purpose to die that we might have life. We confess our sins to You and we rejoice in Your forgiveness. Now empower us so that our gratitude may be translated into service, and more and more of the world's lost may know Your goodness from our lips. In Your strong name. Amen.

Then sing or speak together the following stanzas of "Chief of Sinners Though I Be" (*LW* 285).

Chief of sinners though I be,
Jesus shed His blood for me,
Died that I might live on high,
Lives that I might never die.
As the branch is to the vine,
I am His and He is mine.

Oh, the height of Jesus' love,
Higher than the heav'ns above,
Deeper than the depths of sea,
Lasting as eternity!
Love that found me wondrous thought—
Found me when I sought Him not.

O my Savior help afford
By Your Spirit and Your Word!
When my wayward heart would stray,
Keep me in the narrow way;
Grace in time of need supply
While I live and when I die.

Introduction

In the 1940s and 1950s two diseases—smallpox and polio—received the attention of researchers. Both of these diseases had killed or handicapped hundreds of thousands of Americans, and millions of other people beyond our shores. When vaccines were developed and approved that would prevent these diseases, throngs of people flocked to distribution centers where they could receive these life-giving vaccinations. These vaccines have done their jobs. Both polio and smallpox are under control in this country and in most places throughout the world. But after years of being rid of these menaces because of faithful use of the vaccines, medical researchers

118

now announce that these diseases are again on the rise in some communities. Why? Because of the success of the vaccines, many people have failed to realize that the germ that causes them is still among us. They failed to have their children immunized, and they have fallen prey to the disease that always "prowls around." The victory and security over those diseases is sure, yet some refuse to receive that which is freely given.

1. What is the only vaccine people have been given over sin, death, and the power of the devil?

2. Through faith in Christ God forgives our sins. The Gospel proclaims this healing message of Good News. Why then does it seem that the dreaded and deadly disease—sin—is on the rise in many communities?

3. Health professionals have realized that in this present age they cannot rely on parents to bring their children into the clinic to be immunized. Instead, they must take the vaccine to the people. How is this fact similar to the necessary work of Christ's church today?

Inform

Read each of the three lessons and the short summary of each included here.

Isaiah 43:18–25—These words are addressed to a people that have been a huge disappointment to their God. They, throughout their lives have disobeyed Him. They have mumbled and grumbled. They have looked to foreign gods and foreign priests to assist them in their day-to-day problems. In so doing, they have angered God. God punished them. He sent them into exile both into Assyria and into Babylon. By the time we get to this section of Isaiah's prophesy, Israel is in exile. God proclaims His desire to forgive them, not because of anything they have done, but for His own sake. He assures His people, "I, even I, am He who blots out your transgressions, for My own sake, and remembers your sins no more" (v. 25).

2 Corinthians 1:18–22—Paul speaks of God's faithfulness to the church at Corinth. Paul assures the church that God's promises are always a yes for us in Christ Jesus. God will always enable us to stand firm in Christ and triumph over trouble and division. The Holy Spirit will keep us firm in the faith so that we might receive the guarantee that is to come—eternal life.

Mark 2:1–12—Jesus' ministry has been wonderfully received by the people of Capernaum. He has healed many people and cast out many demons. Upon His return to Capernaum, even more people seek Him for help and healing. There were so many people trying to get to Jesus for help that a group of people who wanted Jesus to heal a paralytic man dragged the man on his stretcher up to the top of the roof and then begin to tear the roof off so that they could lower the man down to Jesus. This was no small feat of engineering. The paralyzed man was lowered through the roof to Jesus. Jesus looks at the man and says, "Son, your sins are forgiven." The teachers of the Law who hear Jesus' words accuse Jesus of blasphemy, "Who can forgive sin but God alone?" Jesus knows what the teachers of the Law are thinking. Jesus asks, "Which is easier: to say to the paralytic, 'Your sins are forgiven,' or to say, 'Get up, take your mat and walk'?" So that people might know that the Son of Man has authority on earth to forgive sins He says to the man, "Get up take up your mat and go home." Jesus makes it clear that He is the Son of God. He has power to forgive sins. He is the Savior of the world. Jesus has come to heal us from our greatest infirmity—sin—so that we might have eternal life.

1. Comment on God's words to Israel, "Forget the former things; do not dwell on the past. See I am doing a new thing!" (v.v. 18–19). In human circles we often hope that people will remember their past indiscretions and the pain they have caused in order that they might be sure to never do those things again. How do God's words differ? What do His words tell us about the forgiveness He provides? What then motivates us who have received His forgiveness through Jesus Christ to do as He desires?

120

2. There will be life in the desert and the inhabitants of the desert will have their lives improved a hundredfold. How does that image relate to those of us who are Christians—people in whom God lives?

3. God, according to Isaiah 43:25 is eager to put our sins out of His memory. What does this say about God's relationship to us? What sorts of things could you "blot out" and so enjoy a better relationship with the people in your life?

4. What does St. Paul mean when he says that God's word to us is always yes and never no?

5. Some people will insist that as Christians we must work hard to obey God in order to earn eternal life. What does 2 Corinthians 1:21–22 say about that?

6. Why is it that most people don't see that the greatest problem we face in life is the one that leads to death without the forgiveness of Christ? What can we do to improve their understanding?

7. A cure for physical and emotional affliction is temporal. A cure for sin is eternal. How might a congregation who focuses all of its attention on healing physical and emotional ailments fail to provide people with their greatest need?

═════════════ **Connect** ═════════════

1. In the lesson from Isaiah, God makes sure that the people of Israel don't ever believe that they somehow have earned His forgiveness. Therefore, after announcing the new day, Isaiah recounts the people's sins. Why is it important today for people to realize that there is nothing they have done to merit God's grace?

2. Isaiah announces that God is doing a new thing. What is the new thing God in Christ Jesus has done in our lives? How does this motivate us to respond in our relationship to God and with our neighbors?

3. Why is it important for the church today to proclaim God's yes? What is the danger of a church that proclaims yes and no? How can we remain certain that what we proclaim is God's yes?

4. What do the crowds that surround Jesus after His first few days in ministry tell us about the needs of people? Do people really know what they need in life? How does this affect the church's mission and ministry?

5. Once a child was born with a serious heart defect. The baby's parents asked for their pastor to come and baptize the baby, and pray over him. The pastor did. After baptizing the baby the pastor prayed, "Lord God, we thank You for the gift of this child and that You have made her Your own eternally through the waters of Baptism. Now we pray, O Lord, that if this child lives one day or a hundred years, it doesn't matter to us, please just see to it that this child lives to Your glory. Amen." Comment on the prayer. Consider Jesus' words in Mark 2:1–12.

══════ **Vision** ══════

During This Week

1. Are there sins from your past that Satan continues to use to plague you? If so, recall Jesus' death on the cross. Then read the words of Isaiah 43:25.
2. Use the word *forgiveness* when you deal with people who have hurt you and apologize. "That's okay" is a common response from people when someone apologizes for hurting them. "You're forgiven" places the offense in its proper context, while providing you the opportunity to testify to the forgiveness you have received through Jesus Christ.
3. Make and send reconciliation cards to people you may be on the "outs" with. In this card let them know that God forgives us so that we can forgive each other. Say in the card, "I forgive you."

Closing Worship

Sing or speak together the following stanzas of "I Lay My Sins on Jesus" (*LW* 366).

I lay my sins on Jesus,
The spotless Lamb of God;
He bears them all and frees us
From the accursed load.
I bring my guilt to Jesus
To wash my crimson stains
Clean in His blood most precious
Till not a spot remains.

I lay my wants on Jesus;
All fullness dwells in Him;
He heals all my diseases;
My soul He does redeem,
I lay my griefs on Jesus,
My burdens and my cares;
He from them all releases;
He all my sorrows shares.

I rest my soul on Jesus,
This weary soul of mine;
His right hand me embraces;
I on His breast recline.
I love the name of Jesus,
Immanuel, Christ, the Lord;
Like fragrance on the breezes
His name abroad is poured.

Scripture Lessons for Next Sunday

Read in preparation for the Eighth Sunday after the Epiphany
Hosea 2:14–16, (17–18,) 19–20; 2 Corinthians 3:1b–6; Mark 2:18–22.

Session 16

Eighth Sunday after the Epiphany

Hosea 2:14–16, (17–18) 19–20; 2 Corinthians 3:1b–6;
Mark 2:18–22

Focus

Theme: *New Wine and New Wineskins*

Law/Gospel Focus

Since the Fall the relationship of creature to Creator has been one of enemy. God sent His Son Jesus into our world to restore the relationship broken between the Creator and the created. Jesus makes us new creatures who live lives that bring glory to God.

Objectives

By the power of the Holy Spirit working through God's Word we will

1. confess the measures to which God would go—sending His only Son to die for us on the cross—to restore the broken relationship that existed between the Creator and the created because of sin;
2. live our lives as a powerful testimony and witness (letter) to God's love for us;
3. express our joy and hope in Christ with people who live without joy and hope.

Opening Worship

Read responsively this paraphrase of Psalm 103:1–12.
Leader: Praise the Lord, O my soul; all my inmost being, praise His holy name.
Participants: Praise the Lord, O my soul, and forget not all His benefits.

Leader: He forgives all my sins and heals all my diseases.

Participants: He redeems my life from the pit and crowns me with love and compassion.

Leader: He satisfies my desires with good things, so that my youth is renewed like the eagle's.

Participants: The Lord works righteousness and justice for all the oppressed.

Leader: He made known His way to Moses, His deeds to the people of Israel.

Participants: The Lord is compassionate and gracious, slow to anger, abounding in love.

Leader: He will not always accuse, nor will He harbor His anger forever.

Participants: He does not treat us as our sins deserve or repay us according to our iniquities.

Leader: For as high as the heavens are above the earth so great is His love for those who fear Him.

Participants: As far as the east is from the west, so far has He removed our transgressions from us.

All: Glory be to the Father and to the Son and to the Holy Spirit; as it was in the beginning is now, and will be forever. Amen.

Introduction

A group of pastors gathered together because of a common concern. They resided in the suburbs outside a major city. Although this city was the home of more than 2 million people, the number of Lutherans in the city had decreased regularly over the past 20 years. The 10 Lutheran congregations located in the city had a combined membership of less than 1,000 people. The pastors sought new ways to reach the area with the Gospel. Since resources were limited, the pastors inquired as to whether one of the congregations would allow itself to be sold, so that resources would be available to support the other congregations. A pastor from the city shared that even though these people were now small in number, they were still very proud. In his estimation none of the congregations would agree to sell their church because of all the memories that the churches held for them.

1. What do you think was the outcome of the meeting?

126

2. How might the suburban congregations be able to assist the city congregations?

3. "Jesus calls us to feed His sheep, not to count them." How might the effectiveness of the ministry of an urban congregation be evaluated if we as Christians embraced the message of this quote?

4. In the Gospel lesson for today Jesus tells the teachers of the Law that the guests do not fast while the bridegroom is with them. There is an urgency because the time will come when the bridegroom will be taken from them. This foreshadows Jesus' death on the cross. Today, as then, there is an urgency to Jesus' message. Jesus will come again to judge the world. Considering this urgency, why do we as a church need to consider our congregations in urban areas important mission stations? What might we do to demonstrate support for urban ministry?

Inform

Read the three Scripture lessons and the brief summaries that follow here.

Hosea 2:14–16,(17–18), 19–20—The people of Israel have involved themselves in idolatry. They are consistently worshiping foreign gods and ignoring the Lord who brought them out of slavery in Egypt. The prophet gets so graphic in his description of their sin that he says they have played the harlot, leaving their husband, God, for other lovers. But amidst the words of judgment are words of hope. In spite of their sin God still loves His people. He explains how He plans to win His people back. God uses the romantic words and themes of a man courting a woman he loved. God will lure her into the desert and there speak tenderly to her. God announces that His renewed relationship with Israel will be characterized as a husband and his betrothed. All the evidence of the old false lovers will be gone forever. From that day on, Israel will be betrothed to God in righteousness and justice forever.

2 Corinthians 3:1b–6—Paul continually suffered the criticism of people opposed to him. His claim to be an apostle was challenged constantly. In the ancient world itinerant preachers like St. Paul would bring letters of recommendation with them as they went from community to community. Paul declares his difference from the other preachers. He needs no letter of recommendation. The Christians he leaves at each place are his letters of recommendation. Paul claims that the people he serves are his letter from Christ Himself. Paul wants to make sure that no one thinks he is boasting. He knows that any success he has had in ministry is not a result of his work or skill but instead is a result of God's power and love. Let it be clearly understood, God has made them competent ministers of a new covenant, a covenant grounded not in Law or letters but in the Spirit of God. It is that Spirit that changes Paul and the people to whom he preaches.

Mark 2:18–22—The teachers of the Law once again are offended by the actions of Jesus' disciples. Jesus and His disciples did not fast. Jesus used the criticism of the teachers of the Law as an opportunity to share with them the difference the Son of God incarnate in the world makes in our observance of Law. The presence of Jesus makes everything and everyone around Him new. He is the bridegroom. Members of the wedding party never fast when the bridegroom is in their midst. Jesus says that He comes to make things and people new.

1. In other translations of Hosea 2:14 the word *allure* is translated "woo." What does the use of this word tell us about God's love and compassion for us?

2. Hosea seems to imply that the days that Israel was in Egypt and their early days in the wilderness were some of the best days she enjoyed with her Lord. Think about some of the things that happened to Israel as they left Egypt and entered the wilderness. What does this say about God's ability to put the best construction on everything?

3. Count the number of times the word *I* is used referring to God in
   Hosea 2:17–20. These verses talk about the salvation of Israel.
   What does the use of this pronoun teach us about the person
   responsible for Israel's salvation? What imagery does Hosea use
   to describe the relationship God will establish between Himself
   and His people?

4. St. Paul says that his detractors may want him to present letters
   of recommendation from other trusted Christian leaders before
   they would believe that he has the authority to preach, teach, and
   direct people as he does. Paul says he needs no letter or recommendation. Instead, the people he has brought to Christ are his
   letter of recommendation. In order to place that statement into
   perspective, think what it would mean if our worth was determined by the behavior of our children? Why can Paul be so con-
   fident in his "children"?

5. Paul's detractors by and large are legalists. They believe that to be
   Christian you also have to keep the Jewish law. What is Paul
   telling his detractors and us when he writes, "He has made us
   competent as ministers of a new covenant—not of the letter but
   of the Spirit; for the letter kills but the Spirit gives life?"

6. What would St. Paul say to the person who claims, "I have decided to follow Jesus?" Consult 2 Corinthians 3:4–5.

7. To what period in the life of Christ does Mark 2:20 refer to? Will the bridegroom ever again be taken from us? What does that suggest about the way we go about living our lives?

8. Jesus said you can't pour new wine into old wineskins without wasting the new wine. If Jesus is the new wine who comes to live in us in love, what is the new wineskin? What does this say about the lives we live as Christians?

Connect

1. Unfaithfulness is one of the major destroyers of marriages in society today. Even faithful Christian people have found themselves betrayed and have been unable to ever trust the unfaithful spouse again. Hosea is clear. Israel has been unfaithful to God. God forgives the unfaithfulness of Israel. God forgives our daily unfaithfulness. Comment on this amazing love and grace. What on earth can compare to it?

2. What got Israel into trouble was their adopting some of the religious traditions of the pagans with whom they lived. For example, fertility rituals seemed to improve their harvests, so they chose to continue trusting in these rituals for help. Are there certain rites and rituals observed by "modern day pagans" that can and do lead Christians astray?

3. God announces through Hosea that in this new day "bow and sword and battle" will be abolished from the land. Today's violence is an indicator of old wine in old wineskins. What is the real hope for peace in the world today?

4. How is your life a letter of your faith in Christ Jesus?

5. How might your congregation be a letter to people in your community who do not know Jesus as their Savior? in the city? in the world?

6. New wine in new wineskins is evidence that Jesus has transformed us. How has your life demonstrated new wine in new wine skins?

Vision

During This Week

1. Be on the lookout for times and ways that you insist that new wine be kept in old wineskins.
2. The Bridegroom is with us. This is a time for joy and hope. Seek new opportunities to express your joy and hope in Christ with those who live without that joy and hope.

Closing Worship

Read responsively Luther's explanation of the significance of Baptism.

Leader: "What does such baptizing with water indicate?"

Participants: "It indicates that the Old Adam in us should by daily contrition and repentance be drowned and die with all sins and evil desires and, that a new man should daily emerge and arise to live before God in righteousness and purity forever."

Leader: "Where is this written?"

Participants: St. Paul writes in Romans chapter six: "We were therefore buried with Him through Baptism into death in order that, just as Christ was raised from the dead through the glory of the Father, we too may live a new life."

Then sing or speak together the following stanzas of "Renew Me, O Eternal Light" (*LW* 373).

> Renew me, O eternal Light,
> And let my heart and soul be bright,
> Illumined with the light of grace
> That issues from Your holy face.
>
> Create in me a new heart, Lord,
> That gladly I obey Your Word.
> Let what You will be my desire,
> And with new life my soul inspire.
>
> Grant that I only You may love
> And seek those things which are above
> Till I behold You face to face,
> O light eternal, through Your grace.

Scripture Lessons for Next Sunday

Read the assigned lessons for The Transfiguration of Our Lord
2 Kings 2:1–12c; 2 Corinthians 3:12–4:2; Mark 9:2–9.

Session 17

The Transfiguration of Our Lord

2 Kings 2:1–12c; 2 Corinthians 3:12–4:2; Mark 9:2–9

Focus

Theme: *Glory to God!*

Law/Gospel Focus

In this sinful world a person's hopes can be easily dashed when looking upon all the trouble and trial that can be experienced in life. In His grace, God breaks through our trouble and trial. He reveals to us His glory in the Word and Sacraments to strengthen our lives so that we might rejoice in the victories that are ours now and are surely ours to come because of Christ our Lord.

Objectives

By the power of the Holy Spirit working through God's Word we will

1. know that trouble and disappointment is a part of all of our lives because of sin in this world;
2. affirm that God in Christ Jesus breaks through our troubles and reveals to us through Word and Sacrament His power and grace, strengthening us to face our future with joy and hope;
3. confess that there is no such thing as a hopeless case or a lost cause in the kingdom of God.

Opening Worship

Sing or speak together "How Good , Lord, to Be Here" (*LW* 89).

How good, Lord, to be here!
Your glory fills the night;
Your face and garments, like the sun,
Shine with unborrowed light.

How good, Lord, to be here,
Your beauty to behold
Where Moses and Elijah stand,
Your messengers of old.

Fulfiller of the past
And hope of things to be!
We hail Your body glorified
And our redemption see.

Before we taste of death,
We see Your kingdom come;
We long to hold the vision bright
And make this hill our home.

Introduction

I came down with polio when I was a young man. Although God has been good to me, and I have lived a very normal life, people still worry about how I might adjust to certain challenges in my life. The greatest example of that concern came during my vicarage. The supervising pastor invited my wife and I to a "welcome" gathering held in our honor. It gave us the opportunity to meet many of the neighboring pastors and some of the leaders of the congregation we would be serving. As I made my way through the crowd meeting folks, I stumbled into the front room and upon a half dozen people sitting on sofas and chairs visiting with one another. I asked if I could join them and happily took a seat. I had no sooner sat down when an elderly man sitting on the sofa said to the person on his left, "Don't you just love the way he walks?" (I walk with a rather pronounced limp.) I thought to myself that I had never met a more rude man in my life. I hoped he would go home soon. No sooner had I thought my thought than he said to a person on the other side of the room, "Don't you just love the way he walks?" I was starting to get angry. I weighed the advantages and disadvantages of chewing this man out in my vicarage supervisor's home, the first time I had been invited there, and decided that discretion was the better part of valor. After a few awkward moments of conversation, the rude man announced that it was in fact time for him to leave. His final remark was directed at me. He said, "I still think you've got one of the best walks I have ever seen." He started on his way and began to walk past me. To my surprise he walked just as I did! He too had polio as a child! He also was a pastor. His whole purpose for being at that gathering was to assure me that a fellow who lived with the effects of polio could indeed put in 40 good years of ministry, just as he had.

1. The experienced pastor wanted to show me that God could and did use those whose bodies were less than perfect. How did God use this aging pastor to give comfort, hope, and courage to the young vicar?

2. Has God ever used a person or event in your life to bring you comfort, hope, and encouragement as you faced challenges? If so, when and how?

3. We may face many challenges in our lives. Sin can place a veil over our lives so that we do not see the glory of God in every event or situation. How can and does God lift the veil from our eyes so that we may see His glory?

In today's lessons—Old Testament and Gospel—God uses extraordinary events in order to reveal His glory to His people who will experience challenges and trials in their lives because of sin. God's revealed glory gives His followers comfort, hope, and encouragement for the future.

Inform

Read each of the lessons assigned for the day and the brief summaries below.

2 Kings 2:1–12—In this section of 2 Kings a transition is made. Politically, King Ahaziah dies and is replaced by King Joram. Spiritually, Elijah is replaced by Elisha. The transition from Elijah to Elisha is carefully documented. When Elijah learns that it is time for him to meet the Lord he begins a last journey. He begins at Gilgal, that place where Israel camped for the first time in the Promised Land, and travels to Bethel. From there he goes southeast 12 miles to Jericho. Along the way he bids farewell to all the prophets in the land. Elisha, probably sensing that this is Elijah's last journey, insists on accompanying him. When they reached the west bank of the Jordan, Elijah struck the water with his cloak and the two crossed over on dry ground. Once there, Elisha asks to be blessed with a double measure of Elijah's spirit and is told that if he sees Elijah go up into heaven then his prayer has been answered. Elisha sees the chariots of fire and horses of fire appear, separating him from Elijah. Elijah goes to heaven in a whirlwind. Elisha has witnessed a powerful demonstration of the glory of God.

2 Corinthians 3:12–4:2—Paul wants his hearers to know that he is living proof that God has established a new and everlasting covenant with his people. It is not like the old covenant made with Moses, the covenant that relied on the letter of the law to bring people to God. This new covenant relies on the Spirit of our Lord Jesus, an enduring and everlasting spirit who transforms sinful human beings into the sons and daughters of God. God's presence in our lives through the new covenant is dependable and permanent. Therefore, Paul can say with confidence, "Since we have such a hope, we are very bold." Now our faces shine in glory for all the world to see. The glory we exude is not from within ourselves but from God. We reflect God's glory. His presence among us and within us enables us to remain steadfast even when we face troubles and challenges. We never lose heart. The glory of God in Christ Jesus has been revealed to us. God gives us everlasting encouragement, hope, and comfort as we face each new day.

Mark 9:2–9—Jesus provides His disciples a vision of power and glory to sustain them during the difficult time to come—Jesus' suffering and death on the cross. Through His power and glory revealed in the Transfiguration, Jesus gives His disciples encouragement, hope, and comfort for the future. The moment was so absolutely splendid that Peter foolishly suggests that they build three tents to contain Jesus, Moses, and Elijah. Jesus lovingly lets Peter know that he has much more important work to do than erecting tents. Instead, Peter will have the important task of sharing the glory of God revealed in the person and work of Jesus with the whole world.

1. Elijah, Elisha, and the prophets in the land all care for each other. What does this suggest about the kind of fellowship we can enjoy in the church? How might this fellowship demonstrate God's glory?

2. Elisha asked for a large blessing from Elijah. Elijah makes it clear that such a request is not his to answers. But he suggests a sign for Elisha so that he will know whether the Lord has heard his prayer and answered it, if God is willing to do a powerful thing for Elisha. What powerful blessings does God give to individuals and His church today so that we might better serve Him?

3. The chariots and horses are a vision of power and might. Do you think that Elisha's ability to see this great sight strengthened him and empowered him? Why? What has God given to us to strengthen and to empower us?

4. Paul tells us that Moses had to veil his face after coming down the mountain because the glory of God that had attached itself to him was too great for the children of Israel to bear. In time, the glory faded away. That is the glory associated with the Law, it is not longstanding. But the glory of the Spirit in the Gospel lasts eternally. What is the difference, then, between the power and glory of the Law and the power and glory of the Gospel?

5. Describe life "in the Spirit" as it is presented by St. Paul.

6. Paul suggests that life in the Spirit of God enables us to live in ways much different from the ways the Law forced us to live. What difference does the Spirit make in our lives and relationships according to 2 Corinthians 4:2?

7. Jesus revealed to Peter, James, and John His glory. What do you think Jesus expected His disciples to do with the experience?

8. Why did God show Moses and Elijah to Jesus and to the disciples? What does the presence of Moses and Elijah tell us about eternal life?

9. Jesus was about to receive a glory greater than the glory He experienced on the Mount of Transfiguration. That moment of true glory would be the moment He hung from the cross, bearing the sins of the world. As He anticipates His crucifixion, God once again announces that "This is my Son, whom I love. Listen to Him!" What counts for real glory according to God?

1. How is the glory of God different from the kind of glory that many people in this day and age seek?

2. God continues to reveal His glory through Word and Sacrament. What activities can people become involved in order to experience God's glory? How can people, in turn, bring glory to God?

3. Because of the glory God has revealed to us, we have such hope that we can be bold in doing the work of our Lord. How can you and/or your congregation demonstrate boldness in doing the Lord's work in your community?

4. St. Paul lets us know that we are being transformed into the likeness of Christ with ever-increasing glory. What evidence is there in your life that God is at work?

Vision

During This Week

1. Think of things that you can do to show forth the true glory of God revealed to you in the person and work of Jesus to other people.
2. Before Elijah ascended into heaven he made sure he said goodbye to all the prophets in his area. This also shows the love and glory of God. Who in your life do you need to speak with, share with, and remind that you care for?

3. Remember the Transfiguration when you face trouble. Remember Jesus has revealed His glory to you so that you may face challenges in your life with comfort, hope, and courage.

Closing Worship

Pray together the Collect for the Transfiguration of our Lord.

O God, in the glorious transfiguration of Your only-begotten Son You once confirmed the mysteries of the faith by the testimony of the ancient fathers, and in the voice that came from the bright cloud You wondrously foreshowed our adoption by grace. Therefore mercifully make us coheirs with our King of His glory, and bring us to the fullness of our inheritance in heaven; through Jesus Christ, our Lord, who lives and reign with You and the Holy Spirit, one God now and forever. Amen.

Scripture Lessons for Next Sunday

Read in preparation for the First Sunday in Lent Genesis 22:1–18; Romans 8:31–39; Mark 1:12–15.